**city o**

# city of peace

## a journey to the roots of my faith

# adrian snell

## charles stewart

MONARCH
Crowborough

**British Library Cataloguing in Publication Data**
A catalogue record for this book is available
from the British Library.

ISBN: 1 85424 290 3

Text typesetting, design and cover artwork
by Jeanette Obbink for The DESIGN Works, Bath
Photograph Adrian Snell on back cover by Gregg, courtesy of
The Leprosy Mission, Peterborough

Produced by Bookprint Creative Services
P.O. Box 827, BN21 3YJ, England for
MONARCH PUBLICATIONS
Broadway House, The Broadway
Crowborough, East Sussex, TN6 1HQ
Printed in Great Britain

# contents

Only the title and page number of books quoted appear in the text. Fuller details are as follows:

*Siddur Sim Shalom* edited by Rabbi Jules (Harlow: The Rabbinical Assembly) 1989 is quoted on pp. 45, 146, 155

*Likrat Shabbat:* Worship, Study and Song for Shabbat and Festival Evenings. Compiled and translated by Rabbi Sidney Greenberg and edited by Rabbi Jonathan D Levine (Prayer Book Press, Media Judaica, Bridgeport, Connecticut, USA). This is quoted on pp. 48, 49, 57, 58, 59

*The Penguin Book of Hebrew Verse* edited and translated by T Carmi (Allen Lane 1981) and reproduced by permission of Penguin Books Ltd. Used on pp. 71, 79, 80. Adrian Snell has adapted these poems in order to set them to music.

*To Be A Jew* by Rabbi Hayim Halevy Donin (Basic Books) 1972 used on p. 97.

*The Light Has Come* Lesslie Newbigin (Hansel Press, Edinburgh) 1982 is quoted on p. 108.

*To Heaven with Scribes and Pharisees* Rabbi Lionel Blue (Darton Longman & Todd ) 1975 is quoted on pp. 131, 132

*A Treasury of Yiddish Poetry* edited by Irving Howe and Eliezer Greenberg (Schocken Books). Copyright applied for and material quoted on pp. 148, 149.

Photographs:
Simon Baker pp. 14, 17, 26, 42, 51, 55, 66, 82, 103, 114, 139
Mariëlle Beekman page 85
Judy Lindeck pp. 20, 33, 39, 62, 70, 79, 110, 122, 129, 130, 150
Jeanette Obbink pp. 23, 104, 142 and all illustrations

Every effort has been made to trace the copyright holders, and any corrections requested will be incorporated into the next printing.

# acknowledgements

Special thanks are due to Walter Riggans for his invaluable comments and support at each stage of the book. To Jeanette Obbink for painstaking attention to every detail of lay-out and design. To Judy Lindeck and Simon Baker for photos that capture in picture what we sought to say in words. To Aad Vermeyden for making sure all was in the right place at the right time!

This book and the albums are dedicated to the Jewish authors down through the centuries who have so immeasurably enriched my life and faith.

# foreword

For Christians and Jews the year 1995-96 has a particular significance because it reminds us that according to tradition it was 3,000 years ago that King David founded the city of Jerusalem. The thoughts and prayers of many will be turning towards the ancient 'city of peace'.

Generally speaking, Christians know little of their indebtedness to their Jewish roots. They scarcely recognise the rock whence they were hewn. The events surrounding the anniversary of Jerusalem's founding should provide us with the opportunity of diminishing our ignorance and increasing mutual understanding.

For many years Adrian Snell has visited Israel, trodden its streets, read its scriptures, absorbed its music and poetry, wrestled with its tragedies, entered into the depths of its longings. Now he has brought his musical skills to help us Christians to appreciate our debt to the Jewish people in his new work, *City of Peace*. In this book, he unfolds some of the words and influences that have challenged and inspired him in his exploration of Jerusalem, its troubled past, its present and its promised future. He helps us listen to the cries of Jewish sages, to face the paradoxes of Jewish history, and to see the hand of God at work.

I hope that through this book we shall understand more clearly what the 'city of peace', which Jesus loved and over which he wept, still has to say to a perplexed world.

Donald Coggan

# introduction

It is now eleven years since I went through the gates of Bergen-Belsen. I shall never forget the experience of that day. It changed me in ways I could not have imagined, not least because it was the first time I had been confronted by the hard questions of the Holocaust.

Those who have listened to my music will know that much of my work over the last ten years has been bound up with my response to the Holocaust, first in *Alpha & Omega* and later in *Song of an Exile*. This musical and spiritual journey has sustained me through times when I have been faced by questions which have no answers. It has helped me to learn not to be afraid of that experience, and also to recognise that my own life, even in times of doubt, failure and struggle, is nevertheless lived with the knowledge of God's faithfulness to me, no matter what.

This journey has also involved me in an increasing awareness of Jewish faith, culture, poetry and experience, which in turn has led to a deep desire to explore the Jewish roots of my Christian faith. In particular, once I began to understand something of the Jewishness of Jesus of Nazareth, Jewish words and understandings started to become an integral part of my own spiritual journey.

The latest stage of this journey has turned my attention to Jerusalem, in Hebrew Yerushalayim, which can be safely translated as 'City of Peace'. Many of the world's great cities conjure up images which transcend the layout in street maps or tourist guides: Rome, the eternal City; Venice, la Serenissima; New York, the Big Apple; Chicago, the Windy City.

But Jerusalem is different. This ancient city, according to tradition captured and established as the Jewish capital by King David 3,000 years ago, is unique in that it is holy to the world's three great monotheistic faiths, Judaism, Christianity and Islam, and remains a central focus of prayer and pilgrimage for all three.

For the Jews, of course, Jerusalem is of paramount importance. Only on the soil of Israel would God's promises to the people Israel come to fruition; only there would they realize their fullest potential as God's people. To those in exile, or later for the Jews of the Diaspora, separation from Jerusalem was almost tantamount to separation from God. Rabbi Hayim Halevy Donin writes: 'There is hardly a religious ritual where Zion is not recalled, where the return to Zion and the restoration and rebuilding of Jerusalem is not mentioned....The *seder* [a festive meal] on the night of Passover ends with the cry *L'shanah habaa b'Yerushalayim* – "Next year in Jerusalem".''

A few years ago I produced an album called *Song of an Exile*, which explored in music what I described then as 'the mystery and the miracle of the Jewish people', through struggle, suffering, exile and the experience of the Holocaust. With the experience of *Song of an Exile* still very much with me, I found myself wanting to explore the mystery and the meaning of Jerusalem. How could 'City of Peace' be applied to this particular city, which has probably known more war and destruction than any other city in human history? Seven times it has been destroyed and rebuilt. And yet contained within the name of the city there is a promise which I find at once perplexing and exciting.

The outcome is a new work called *City of Peace* in which I have tried to give musical expression to my reflections on this holiest of cities. This book is a further outworking of those ideas. For readers who have heard the music, it will explain some of the thinking behind the notes, but it can be read just as easily by those who have never heard the piece.

All of the texts used in *City of Peace* are drawn from Jewish sources, whether Biblical or beyond, whether Old Testament prophecies, words of Yeshua (Jesus), or contemporary Jewish poetry. These different strands are integrated in the hope that they may have something to contribute to our understanding of the whole. At the end of most chapters there will also be some further material to help those to would like to reflect on some of the issues raised, and particularly for those who want to combine the reading of this book with listening to the music of *City of Peace*.

I am overwhelmingly grateful to Charles Stewart for his willingness as friend and fellow pilgrim to undertake the enormous task of articulating my story. Through hours of taped conversations, exchanges over the telephone, reams of written material and numerous listenings to the albums, he has managed to faithfully convey my mind and heart over these matters.

Adrian

*The old city*

# chapter **one**

In each of my visits to Jerusalem I have been struck by the impact of this ancient, yet contemporary, city and by the way it seems to hold the pilgrim in its embrace. Yerushalayim is a place where history, culture and faith come together. The smells of the spices and herbs in the markets, the tastes and the colours - all contribute to the multinational flavour of a city whose inhabitants are now drawn from every continent on earth. It is beautiful, vibrant and alive; and though sometimes the tensions and the sense of struggle are palpable, yet there is also a powerful impression that this is a city with a future.

It is also a place with incredible roots. Behind the contemporary city are 3,000 years of hopes, fears and yearnings for Jerusalem. This city has been prophesied over more than any other in world history, and many of those promises and prophecies have yet to be fulfilled. Within the close, confined spaces of the Old City, where children still tumble over each other in narrow streets and the crowds jostle past the traders in the gate, the central events of the Christian faith took place. This was the city that Jesus entered on his Palm Sunday procession from the Mount of Olives. He healed people in its streets and he taught in the Temple. This was where he overturned the tables of the money-changers. He was arrested, tried and crucified here. This was where he rose from the dead.

One of the things I hope to achieve through the music of *City of Peace* is to show how many aspects of Jerusalem's story can connect with the individual believer, at whatever point in history that believer lives. Faith and faithlessness, rebellion, betrayal, exile, separation from God, promises of reconciliation – so many of these things which are part of human experience are written into the stones of this city. This is not to say that all these things are necessarily part of the New Testament story, but if we are unaware of those experiences and their place in salvation history then inevitably our understanding of Jesus, and the culture in which he came to birth, will be diminished. Indeed, if we can only begin to think of Jesus as Yeshua, the name by which his family and his disciples addressed him, we shall have taken an important step towards a fuller understanding of the person and the teaching of the Lord we worship. We shall also have identified ourselves more closely with Messianic Jews, those within the Jewish community who believe in Yeshua as Messiah and King.

Of course, our Christian faith in God and our knowledge of God's gracious dealings with us involves us in much more than Jerusalem, the Jewish people, and the land of Israel. But until those Jewish roots become part of the foundation of our Christian faith, then we are depriving ourselves of so much of what God has revealed of himself and his age-long love for humanity. I long for us to rediscover the mystery and excitement, the sheer 'earthedness' of all this; and from there to go on to ask again the central questions of Christian faith and life, with our understanding of God and his purposes for salvation newly and immeasurably enriched.

Anyone with an eye for the news will appreciate the extent to which Jerusalem continues to be a city of contention. It would be all too easy to let this present reality dominate *City of Peace*, and so cloud the deeper issues which we're trying to address. My primary aim is to look beyond the present realities to the deeper reality which is in God and comes from God. The perspec-

*The many faces of Jerusalem*

tive here is not that of time-bound human experience, but is rather the perspective of eternity. It's not that I want to ignore the present day issues, or the social and political realities of contemporary Israel – inevitably, they will arise from time to time – but I want to see these issues within a wider context. Then this deeper reality becomes not only Israel's story, but our story too.

## Prayer for Travellers

I first encountered these words during a visit to Israel, when I found them written in the inside cover of a book. At the time, I thought it a beautiful expression of the deep-seated human desire for God's blessing and protection on all the journeys of life, whether physical or spiritual.

*May the God who called our father Avraham*

*Avinu Avraham, Avinu Avraham, Avinu, Avinu.*

*You called him to journey into the unknown*

*And you guarded him and you blessed him,*

*Protect me too,*

*Bless me too.*

*May his spirit be with me on the way,*

*May he lead me home in peace,*

*Back to my home in peace.*

Adapted from the *Jewish Prayer Book*

As I reflected on the prayer, it struck me that there could be no better focus for this prayer than Abraham – Avraham in Hebrew. The story of Yerushalayim begins with God's call to the 75-year old Abram (as he was then called) to make a journey, to pack up his bags, leave behind his home and all he knew, and set off into the unknown. This journey led him first to Canaan, then on to Egypt to escape a severe famine. Later it was to lead him back to Canaan, and eventually after many years to Mount Moriah and to the supreme test of his faith. Twenty-four years after God's first call to Abraham, the promises were confirmed:

*The Judean Desert*

*As for me, this is my covenant with you: You will be the father of many nations. No longer will you be called Abram [i.e. 'exalted father']; your name will be Abraham [i.e. 'father of many nations'] , for I have made you a father of many nations. I will make you very fruitful; I will make nations of you, and kings will come from you. I will establish my covenant as an everlasting covenant between me and you and your descendants after you for the generations to come, to be your God and the God of your descendants after you. The whole land of Canaan, where you are now an alien, I will give as an everlasting possession to you and your descendants after you; and I will be their God.* (Genesis 17.3-8)

Perhaps the most remarkable thing about this journey was that Abraham set off not knowing the final destination. He was only told: 'Go from your country and your father's house to the land that I will show you.' That demanded a constant openness to the God who had called him, and who had promised to bless him and make him a blessing to others.

When I showed the words of this prayer to my friend and colleague Richard Ayal Frieden – a Messianic Jew and dancer living in Israel who has performed with me often – I was intrigued by the response. Richard smiled with the joy of recognition and told me that this is the kind of prayer contemporary Israelis might have on their car dashboard, as a prayer to use just before setting out on a journey: 'protect me too, bless me too.'

In thinking about Richard's response, it became clearer to me that there were many points of connection between 'our father Abraham' and God's people today. Not that the connection depends on making a physical journey. That would be to restrict Abraham's relevance to those fortunate enough to have followed in his footsteps, or who have made a pilgrimage to Israel. But Abraham's relevance is for all God's people, not for the few. Of course, it is not difficult to discover a special sense of God's presence when on a formal pilgrimage. Indeed part of the intention behind any pilgrimage is the desire to meet with God in special places where, in T S Eliot's telling phrase, 'prayer has been valid'. Even the relative discomfort of travel can contribute to this sense of God's presence, though nowadays we are more likely to be crammed into narrow-seated planes or in buses with broken-down air-conditioning, than face the rigours and dangers experienced by earlier pilgrims.

It is much harder to realize a sense of being on a spiritual journey within the everyday setting of our lives, in which routine activities and worries can so easily crowd out the awareness of God's presence. We may 'go on pilgrimage' in an attempt to make sense of what is happening in that everyday life, but if we are to encounter God here and now, then the more important spiritual journey will be the one we undertake every day where we are, at home, at work, in the community. That is the context in which Jesus' call to 'follow me' will be lived out.

We forget that it was no different in biblical times. Despite our familiarity with the stories of the great heroes of faith, we tend to think of their lives as one climactic incident after another, one moment of profound revelation followed by a moment of terrible despair. But those are only the parts of the story we read about: what happened all the other days? Even Abraham had to encounter God in the humdrum events of life, and not only in the giving of the covenant or the near-sacrifice of Isaac on Mount Moriah.

If we can learn to recognise our lives as being a perpetual 'pilgrimage in ordinary', then Abraham's journey can be seen as a metaphor for the journey of our lives, with all their

uncertainty and unpredictability. Changes of home, changes of job and career, all the potential for personal tragedy and opportunity, for hopes and fears: who knows what we might face? Our future is every bit as unknowable as Abram's when he set off to follow the call of the Lord. Perhaps we can make this prayer ours, too: 'Lord, my life is a journey; be with me as you were with Abraham, as I go forward into the unknown; protect me too, bless me too; and lead me back home in peace.'

If Abraham's journey can be a metaphor for our lives, it also serves as a metaphor for Jerusalem itself, for the city itself is on another kind of static pilgrimage. Ever since the momentous test of Abraham's faith on Mount Moriah, God's purposes of salvation have been intimately bound up with this place: the foundation of the city by David three thousand years ago, the building of Solomon's temple, the bitter history of exile and return, the coming of Jesus and the promise of the Kingdom. Since the birth of Jesus the city has experienced destruction by the Romans, nearly 2,000 years of further turmoil, and in this century the formation of the State of Israel in 1948 and the reunification of Jerusalem under Israeli control in 1967.

*City of Peace* explores this journey, from the journey of Abraham the traveller to the coming of the New Jerusalem promised in the Revelation to John. For some, this may be a journey into new territory. Exploring some of the roots of Christian faith may lead us to confront and question borrowed assumptions or hand-me-down generalizations about Judaism, the nation and the culture which gave birth to Jesus of Nazareth. But the God who called Abraham to launch out into the unknown and guided him and guarded him, will be with us also as we venture on in our pilgrimage of discovery. Like Abraham, we need not fear what we shall encounter on the way.

# For Reflection

## A Pilgrim's Prayer

Yeshua, you are the way, the truth and the life.
May we who tread in your earthly footsteps
not wander from your way of holiness.
Faring forth in your blessed company,
may we feel our hearts burn within us
and know you face to face at our journey's end.

Source unknown

# For Listening

## Prayer for Travellers CD1

*View from the Mount of Olives*

# chapter **two**

One of the first tasks of any pilgrim to Jerusalem is to make the journey to the top of the Mount of Olives, and from there to look across the Kedron Valley to the heart of the Old City, known to Jews and Christians as Temple Mount and to Muslims as the *Haram esh Sharif*, or 'Noble Sanctuary'. Where today we see the Al-Aqsa Mosque and the splendour of the golden Dome of the Rock, in earlier days stood the Temple where Jesus worshipped and taught.

Like most children brought up in Christian families, I first heard the name Jerusalem at an early age. The name was familiar from Bible stories, and I probably tried to imagine Jesus walking the city streets or worshipping in the Temple. Whatever mental images I'd adopted or inherited, it was only when I went to Jerusalem for the first time that I came to appreciate the nature of the Old City which Jesus knew, and to realize that the city in which the central events of salvation history took place is an area no larger than the size of an English mediaeval market town.

The more I thought about Jerusalem, and about the Jewish faith, history and culture with which it is bound up, the more it became clear that, like most Western Christians, I'd had a tendency to think that Christianity began with Jesus' birth in the stable. I didn't really know what came before or, if I did, I hadn't made the connection, and so had effectively divorced Jesus from his roots and from the traditions of his people. What I had not realized was the extent to which this had impoverished my understanding of Jesus, and what he said and did.

The effect of seeing these sites of special meaning over several years has been to see the person of Jesus in a new light and to discover the importance of spiritual roots located in a place – specifically in this place, Jerusalem. Being a musician, it was only natural that my response to this place, to this most complex of cities, would be through music. The result is my new work, called *City of Peace*.

Paradoxically, as I have learned that my Christian faith is deeply rooted in this city, so I have been set free to live with a different kind of rootedness whether at home with my family in Bath, or on tour, or wherever I am.

This approach to thinking about Jesus, his city, his people and his nation, has opened up for me new areas of exploration and study, and has begun to make sense of things that Christians have so often succeeded in making no sense of, precisely because we so often try to comprehend the most significant moment in the story of salvation without any real sense of its context. I have come to realize that so long as we divorce Christian faith from those roots, our faith will always tend to be unbalanced, over-spiritualized, and far from the wholeness of life which Jesus came to bring.

•••••

A few hundred yards down from the crest of the Mount of Olives stands a church in the shape of a tear-drop. Designed by Barluzzi – the noted 20th century Italian architect who also designed the octagonal church on the Mount of the Beatitudes overlooking the Sea of Galilee – it marks the spot where,

according to tradition, Jesus wept over the city.   Hence the
Latin name of the church:  Dominus Flevit - the Lord wept.

*As he approached Jerusalem and saw the city, he wept over it*
*and said, 'If you, even you, had only known on this day what would*
*bring you peace – but now it is hidden from your eyes.  The days will*
*come upon you when your enemies will build an embankment against*
*you and encircle you and  hem you in on every side.  They will dash*
*you to the ground, you and the  children within your walls. They will*
*not leave one stone on another, because you did not recognize the time*
*of God's coming to you.'* (Luke 19.41-44)

Knowing Jerusalem's history as he knew it, knowing what
was to happen to him there only a few days later, and knowing
something of its future until his return,  how else could Jesus
have reacted except with such sorrow and yearning?

This image of Jesus weeping over the city was my
starting point in the original conception of *City of Peace*, in a
song based on Luke 13.34-35 and Matthew 11.17, and entitled
*'O Yerushalayim'*.

*O Yerushalayim, Yerushalayim,*
*I played a flute for you*
*but you did not dance, you did not dance.*

*O Yerushalayim, Yerushalayim,*
*I sang a dirge for you*
*but you did not weep, you did not weep.*

*O Yerushalayim, Yerushalayim,*

*How often have I longed*

*to gather your children together.*

*But you were not willing,*

*you would not have me.*

*I tell you, you shall not see me, till you hear*

*Baruch HaBa B'Shem Adonai*

*'Blessed is he who comes in the name of the Lord'*

based on Luke 13.34-35 and Matthew 11.17

One of things I try to convey in this song is the recurring contrariness inherent in Jerusalem. This is the Holy City in which prophets are killed. This is the city which looked for the coming of the Messiah, and prayed for his coming in the Temple and particularly in the great religious festivals; but when he was born, 'he came to that which was his own, and his own did not receive him' (John 1.11).

From any rational perspective it was surely foolish of God to choose as the 'City of God' a hill town surrounded by wilderness, without much in the way of food resources, always at risk of attack because of its proximity to the main trade routes from Asia to Egypt, and perpetually beset by serious problems of water supply. But the foolishness of God is a frequent biblical theme. Think of the folly of God's choice of Abraham, an old man married to a barren wife long past child-bearing years, to be the father of a nation. What folly to select any race – no more rebellious, no less repentant, than any other, but as fallibly human as the rest of us – to be specially chosen as the means by which the whole world would come to learn about God. What folly to send the Messiah as a human baby, weak, desperately vulnerable, born of an unmarried mother in a smelly Judaean stable underneath the inn.

But if the geographical location of God's city was foolish, how much more foolish was the name: Yerushalayim, the City of Peace. Have there been many periods when it has been a city at peace? How can we come to terms with the paradox of this city whose name implies wholeness, yet which is divided formally along ethnic and religious lines into Quarters, and whose centuries-long brokenness is written in blood. The paradox reaches even to the Church of the Holy Sepulchre, whose immense spaces cover the most strongly authenticated sites of Calvary and the empty tomb. Even here, in what should be the point of greatest Christian unity on earth, representatives of different Christian denominations maintain an uneasy truce, each looking to their own interests, each wary of their neighbours.

However, I believe that the brokenness which is the reality of Jerusalem today is not the whole story, and that we must strive to see that apparent reality in the light of the promise which was given in the beginning. We must hold fast to that promise, for without it we may see only the suspicion, fear, passion and hostility which sometimes seem endemic in Jerusalem today. Without the vision, we may lose sight of the hope of final redemption which God has promised.

The paradox of a City of Peace which knows no peace is not solved by seeing only the bustling, troubled, contemporary city, nor by over-spiritualizing the issues raised by Jerusalem today. Holding God's words of promise along side the Jerusalem of the news bulletins will not be easy.

The image of Jesus weeping over the city takes us right to

*Inside the Church of the Holy Sepulchre*

the heart of the relationship between God and Jerusalem. Indeed, to read Jesus' words from the gospels while looking across the Kedron valley is to glimpse the timeless longing of God to reach out in love and bring his people home. The God of all creation, transcendent, immeasurably powerful, cares for his people with the tenderness of a protective mother. This is the God who, over centuries, patiently taught his people about himself and the way he wanted them to live.

This is the God who sent his only Son to redeem the world and whose Spirit points people of all nationalities and races to Jesus the Christ, Yeshua Ha-Moshiach. And I believe God still cries over Jerusalem, and over a world where so many will not listen to his word, follow his ways, or run to his arms to receive his love and embrace his shalom.

# For Reflection

## A Prayer for Peace in the Holy Land

O Lord, soften the stone hearts
of those who preach and practice
intolerance and bigotry;
as the sun's setting glow
softens the stone walls
of your Holy City, Jerusalem.

Lord, the rocky hills, the valleys,
the deserts and the sea shore
are filled with the echoes of
centuries of pain.

Lord, bring peace to house and village.
Comfort the mothers who fret and those who mourn.
Lord, keep strong the twisted old root
of the olive tree,
and protect the young vine.

Lord of water and stone,
of bread and wine,
Lord of resurrection,
feed hope, and bring peace
to this racked but beautiful holy land.

Gerald Butt *Source unknown*

# For Listening

## Over the city CD1

The serene confidence of the title track gives way to instrumental music which seeks to express God's sorrow over the city and over the world. Somehow, the city of peace (in Hebrew, *shalom*) has become a place of estrangement and exile. The wordless crying which sounds over instrumental chords is akin to the 'sighs too deep for words' of which Paul writes in Romans 8.26, as the Holy Spirit sings the pain-racked sighs of a God who loves all that he has made, but cannot prevent humanity from going wrong, with disastrous results for creation, for his people, and for Jerusalem.

## O Yerushalayim CD1

The music of this song reflects the history of Jerusalem from its foundation to the present. The use of the harp is a musical reminder of David, the harp-playing shepherd who became king and established Jerusalem as the capital of his kingdom. The words of Jesus were spoken days before the forces of darkness were routed for ever by his crucifixion just outside the city wall, and resurrection from Joseph of Arimathea's tomb in the garden nearby. The introduction, played by the flute, is a melody characteristic of Middle-Eastern music today.

# chapter **three**

*Walk with the words of life all around you,*
*all shall be filled with the joy of your faithfulness.*

So many of our perceptions of Jerusalem derive either from contemporary news of communal unrest and violence or from the stories of spiritual conflict in the Bible. I believe we should remember that none of these conflicts were God's intention either for the place or for the people. From the beginning, God made provision for all that was necessary for their life to be ordered aright. He gave them a Covenant, as a sign that they belonged; he gave them Commandments to guide them in the right paths; and he gave them a place where they could be at home.

We usually think of the Covenant (not unnaturally) in solemn terms. But alongside the solemnity, God's Covenant with Abraham was meant to bring joyful, vibrant life. I wanted to convey something of this in an interpretation of the Covenant, based on a number of passages from Genesis, which I incorporated as the second song of *City of Peace*. This song contains several ideas which have been very important to my thinking, particularly in attempting to set out God's vision and purpose for Yerushalayim.

*Lift up your eyes, for as far as you see,*
*To the north, to the south, to the west and the east*
*Is the land that is promised to you and your children*
*A place to belong and to live in shalom.*

*Take your sons and your daughters and follow my way*
*Learn to love my commandments, my laws to obey*
*And I'll make your name great,*
*I will bless those who bless you*
*I'll curse those who mock and despise and deride you.*

*All shall be bathed in your light and your fragrance*
*All shall be filled with the joy of your faithfulness.*

*Care for this world of such beauty and wonder,*
*Guard my creation, respect one another.*
*For I am your shield, your defender, your Lord;*
*This is my promise, this my reward.*

based on passages from Genesis

First (in order of appearance rather than importance) there is the 'looking up' which is so familiar from the Psalms:

*I lift up my eyes to the hills - where does my help come from? My help comes from the Lord who made heaven and earth* (Psalm 121.1-2).

The more I read in the Hebrew Bible, and especially in the Psalms, the more this idea leaps off the page as a recurring theme for the people of Israel. Take, for example, Psalms 120-134, the Songs of Ascents, which were sung by God-fearing Jews as they came up to Jerusalem for the great religious festivals of the Jewish year. The climb which this involved was a powerful symbol of their aspirations, of the call to look up in heart and spirit to God, and to that 'something better' which is

*Golden Gate*

with God. That these aspirations were so closely linked with the Feasts of the Covenant, the seasonal reminders of God's grace and goodness in the past, only emphasised the people's continuing need to depend on him in the present.

Secondly, there is the land itself:

> *To the north, to the south, to the west and the east,*
> *Is the land that is promised to you and your children*

Today, the whole question of the land and its possession is a vexed political issue, both within Israel and internationally, an issue so complicated by the claims and counter-claims of Palestinians and Jews that it is virtually impossible to consider it dispassionately. We'll return to that later. For now, I simply want to register the importance of the land - of this particular land - to the people of Israel in Biblical times. It was the place promised to them by God, and they knew it as their first real homeland. Even the bitter experience of years of exile in Babylon only reinforced the love of the Jewish people for their homeland, and especially for Jerusalem itself:

> *If I forget you, O Jerusalem, may my right hand forget its skill.*
> *May my tongue cling to the roof of my mouth if I do not remember you,*
> *if I do not consider Jerusalem my highest joy.*　　　(Ps 137. 5-6)

When I think of the passions aroused so easily in Britain today by what some perceive as European threats to our currency and sovereignty, then I begin to understand the fervour of those Jews in the 6th century B.C. who had been exiled from their land and had seen Jerusalem destroyed.

Then there is the many-layered word 'shalom', which is normally translated as 'peace', though its range of meaning

includes a sense óf deep spiritual well-being, of wholeness,
completeness, and the inner security which comes only from
knowledge of God and the salvation he brings. For me, one of
the most powerful depictions of what shalom means comes in
the prophet Micah:

*They will beat their swords into ploughshares and their spears
into pruning hooks. Nation will not take up sword against nation,
nor will they train for war any more. Every man will sit under his
own vine and under his own fig tree, and no one will make them
afraid, for the Lord Almighty has spoken.* (Micah 4. 3-4)

*Signs of life and hope*

Although the word shalom doesn't actually appear in that passage, it infuses every phrase and image. To sit under their fig tree, at peace in the place of promise where they belong, a place where fear is a stranger: a powerful picture which speaks to the universal human longing to belong somewhere and to someone, in this case to belong in this tiny land at the eastern end of the Mediterranean Sea and to the God who led them there. That promise of shalom and of perfect 'at-home-ness' is contained within the Covenant. When we can say 'He is my God, I am his, and I am in the place God wants me to be', then, no matter how imperfectly it is realized, his shalom is present. The presence of perfect shalom is part of God's vision for Yerushalayim, and will one day transform the 'City of Peace' from a dream to a reality.

Another crucial theme, which appears in the second verse of *The Covenant*, is the two-way relationship between God and his people:

*Take your sons and your daughters and follow my way*

*Learn to love my commandments, my laws to obey*

*And I'll make your name great,*

*I will bless those who bless you*

*I'll curse those who mock and despise and deride you.*

In other words, God promises to love and bless his people, and to shower them with his grace, freely given. Israel is called to respond by loving God, and accepting his grace by obeying the laws which he has given them.

*And now, O Israel, what does the Lord your God ask of you but to fear the Lord your God, to walk in all his ways, to love him, to serve*

*the Lord your God with all your heart and with all your soul, and to*
*observe the Lord's commands and decrees that I am giving you today*
*for your own good?* (Deuteronomy 10.12-13)

Just as in the great Commandment, love for God is linked inextricably to love for neighbour, so this idea of mutual love spills over into other relationships:

> *Care for this world of such beauty and wonder,*
> *Guard my creation, respect one another.*

Respect for each other, and respect for the creation into which God has placed us: two aspects of one of the most profound commands given by God to his creatures. It is of special relevance today, when so many human relationships are breaking down because of lack of mutual respect and where lack of care for the creation has led to so many actual and potential environmental disasters.

> *All shall be bathed in your light and your fragrance*
> *All shall be filled with the joy of your faithfulness.*

The vital word here is 'all'. Yes, the Covenant given by God to Abraham is rooted specifically in this people, and rooted in the promised land. But from the start, the Covenant contained the promise that through this people all nations would be blessed. This Covenant, and its promises of blessing, are ultimately for everyone. This is God's Covenant with all humanity, which was to reach its climax in the birth, ministry, death and resurrection of Yeshua.

# For Reflection

**A prayer** from the Jewish weekday morning service

**Master of all worlds!** Not upon our merit do we rely in our supplication, but upon Your limitless love. What are we? What is our life? What is our piety? What is our righteousness? What is our attainment, our power, our might? What can we say, Lord our God and God of our ancestors? Compared to You, the mighty are nothing, the famous nonexistent, the wise lack wisdom, the clever lack reason. For most of their actions are meaningless, the days of their lives emptiness. Human pre-eminence over beasts is an illusion when all is seen as futility.

But we are Your people, partners to Your covenant, descendants of Your beloved Abraham to whom You made a pledge on Mount Moriah. We are heirs of Isaac, his son bound upon the altar. We are your firstborn people, the congregation of Isaac's son Jacob whom You named Israel and Jeshurun, because of Your love for him and Your delight in him. Therefore it is our duty to thank You and praise You, to glorify you and sanctify Your name. How good is our portion, how pleasant our lot, how beautiful our heritage. How blessed are we that twice each day, morning and evening, we are privileged to declare:

**Hear O Israel: The Lord our God, the Lord is one.**
Praised be his glorious sovereignty throughout all time.

From *Siddur Sim Shalom,* pp 13-15

# For Listening

## The Covenant  CD1

שְׁמַע יִשְׂרָאֵל יְהוָה אֱלֹהֵינוּ יְהוָה אֶחָד׃ וְאָהַבְתָּ אֵת
יְהוָה אֱלֹהֶיךָ בְּכָל־לְבָבְךָ וּבְכָל־נַפְשְׁךָ וּבְכָל־מְאֹדֶךָ׃
וְהָיוּ הַדְּבָרִים הָאֵלֶּה אֲשֶׁר אָנֹכִי מְצַוְּךָ הַיּוֹם עַל־
לְבָבֶךָ׃ וְשִׁנַּנְתָּם לְבָנֶיךָ וְדִבַּרְתָּ בָּם בְּשִׁבְתְּךָ בְּבֵיתֶךָ
וּבְלֶכְתְּךָ בַדֶּרֶךְ וּבְשָׁכְבְּךָ וּבְקוּמֶךָ׃ וּקְשַׁרְתָּם לְאוֹת
עַל־יָדֶךָ וְהָיוּ לְטֹטָפֹת בֵּין עֵינֶיךָ׃ וּכְתַבְתָּם עַל־מְזוּזֹת
בֵּיתֶךָ וּבִשְׁעָרֶיךָ׃

שְׁמַע יִשְׂרָאֵל יְהוָה אֱלֹהֵינוּ יְהוָה אֶחָד׃ וְאָהַבְתָּ אֵת
יְהוָה אֱלֹהֶיךָ בְּכָל־לְבָבְךָ וּבְכָל־נַפְשְׁךָ וּבְכָל־מְאֹדֶךָ׃
וְהָיוּ הַדְּבָרִים הָאֵלֶּה אֲשֶׁר אָנֹכִי מְצַוְּךָ הַיּוֹם עַל־
לְבָבֶךָ׃ וְשִׁנַּנְתָּם לְבָנֶיךָ וְדִבַּרְתָּ בָּם בְּשִׁבְתְּךָ בְּבֵיתֶךָ
וּבְלֶכְתְּךָ בַדֶּרֶךְ וּבְשָׁכְבְּךָ וּבְקוּמֶךָ׃ וּקְשַׁרְתָּם לְאוֹת
עַל־יָדֶךָ וְהָיוּ לְטֹטָפֹת בֵּין עֵינֶיךָ׃ וּכְתַבְתָּם עַל־מְזוּזֹת
בֵּיתֶךָ וּבִשְׁעָרֶיךָ׃

שְׁמַע יִשְׂרָאֵל יְהוָה אֱלֹהֵינוּ יְהוָה אֶחָד׃ וְאָהַבְתָּ אֵת
יְהוָה אֱלֹהֶיךָ בְּכָל־לְבָבְךָ וּבְכָל־נַפְשְׁךָ וּבְכָל־מְאֹדֶךָ׃
וְהָיוּ הַדְּבָרִים הָאֵלֶּה אֲשֶׁר אָנֹכִי מְצַוְּךָ הַיּוֹם עַל־
לְבָבֶךָ׃ וְשִׁנַּנְתָּם לְבָנֶיךָ וְדִבַּרְתָּ בָּם בְּשִׁבְתְּךָ בְּבֵיתֶךָ
וּבְלֶכְתְּךָ בַדֶּרֶךְ וּבְשָׁכְבְּךָ וּבְקוּמֶךָ׃ וּקְשַׁרְתָּם לְאוֹת
עַל־יָדֶךָ וְהָיוּ לְטֹטָפֹת בֵּין עֵינֶיךָ׃ וּכְתַבְתָּם עַל־מְזוּזֹת
בֵּיתֶךָ וּבִשְׁעָרֶיךָ׃

# chapter **four**

While the Covenant with Abraham was the starting point of the relationship between God and the Jewish people, the daily renewal of that Covenant finds its greatest expression in these timeless words :

*Shema Yisrael, Adonai Elohainu, Adonai Ehad.*

*Hear, O Israel: The Lord our God, the Lord is One.*

With the *Shema* we come to the heart of Judaism. Christians know these words as part of the Great Commandment which Jesus confirmed in Mark 12.29:

*One of the teachers of the Law came and heard them debating. Noticing that Jesus had given them a good answer, he asked him, 'Of all the commandments, which is the most important?' 'The most important one,' answered Jesus, ' is this: "Hear, O Israel, the Lord our God, the Lord is one. Love the Lord your God with all your heart and with all your soul and with all your mind and with all your strength'" The second is this: "Love your neighbour as yourself". There is no commandment greater than these.* (Mark 12.29)

It was necessary for *City of Peace* to include a setting of the *Shema*. How could I explore the Jewish roots of Christian faith without exploring the Jewish roots of Jewish faith? For Jesus, clearly, the *Shema* was at the heart of what it meant to worship the living God. 2,000 years on, it is still impossible to over-estimate the importance of these words to the God-fearing Jew.

*The best known prayer of Judaism is: 'Hear, O Israel: the Lord our God, the Lord is one.' This prayer makes no request of God. It only affirms that God is one. Its recital is not needed by God; He does not need to be reminded that He is One. It is needed by us; we must be reminded that God is one. We must be reminded that only God is to be worshipped, or else we might worship idols or power or wealth or prestige or the other false gods which easily claim people today, as three thousand years ago. To worship something means to give everything one possesses, all one's talents and energies to this end.... Thus, twice daily, we recite the* Shema *so that we may be reminded that there is but One God in the universe to whom we should dedicate everything we possess.*

Ferdinand M. Isserman , from *Likrat Shabbat,* p 68

In other words, the *Shema* is not really a prayer at all. These words are a declaration of faith which gives the context for all other prayers, and makes prayer possible. Twice a day, morning and evening, every Jew is required to recite the *Shema,* in affirmation of the unity of God of heaven and earth and as a reminder of their obligations to Him.

Nahum Waldman's paraphrase of the *Shema* elaborates some of its main ideas:

### 'These words....'
Let us commit our hearts and might
to accept in love the kingship of heaven,
to do that which is expected of us,
to live the covenant day and night.

### 'HEAR'
Let not egotism, personal or national, seal our ears
to the cry for compassion or the voice of divine command.

### 'O ISRAEL'

We are linked by a bond we are not free to break.
We are of the covenant people whose ancestors
heard God's voice, whose prophets beheld him in visions.
We have been compared to the lamb, torn by vicious wolves,
and to the lion, unafraid to walk alone among the peoples

### 'THE LORD OUR GOD'

In a pagan world which treated humans as divine
and adored gods with the vices of humans,
our people stood apart, witnesses to a daring faith:
The God of holiness, who loves us,
demands justice and mercy;
He will, one day, be the God of all humanity.

### 'THE LORD IS ONE'

The universe,
its diversity, complexity, and seeming contradictions,
all derive from one source, the One Creator.
People, unlike by history, race, and temperament,
are yet of one family, the children of One Father.
He is the King, and his kingship is not in a far-off age;
it is in us, and upon us, if we will now accept its yoke.

From *Likrat Shabbat,* p 70

What is clear from the passage immediately after the first appearance of the *Shema* is that God knew it was not enough to give his people that fundamental credal statement. It was also vitally important to teach them how to implement and develop those words in everyday living.

*Hear, O Israel: The Lord our God, the Lord is One. Love the Lord your God with all your heart and with all your soul and with all your strength. These commandments that I give you today are to be upon your hearts. Impress them on your children. Talk about them when you sit at home and when you walk along the road, when you lie down and when you get up. Tie them as symbols on your hands and bind them on your foreheads. Write them on the door-frames of your houses and on your gates.* (Deuteronomy 6.4-9)

When we unpack these verses, we begin to see how carefully and graciously God was guiding his people. The Israelites are to impress God's commandments on their children; this ensured that the principles enshrined in the *Shema* would enter the fabric of family life, and would provide continuity into the next generation.

I see something of what this means in practice, whenever I stay in Jerusalem with Richard Ayal Frieden and his wife, Yardena. In common with other Messianic Jewish families, they worship Yeshua while at the same time retaining their Jewish heritage. I see how their son Roie is being brought up. As Yardena lights the candles at dusk at the beginning of *Shabbat* (Sabbath), so there beings a demonstration of how their faith is expressed through the everyday events of family life. That life, as with any believing Jewish family, is shot through with symbolic actions which serve as constant reminders of God, his love and his salvation.

By contrast, I feel the way *we* pass on the faith is much less centred on the home, which leave me with a deep sense of inadequacy. Is it any wonder that so many children of Christian families grow up with such a confused picture of faith? Sunday lunch is still a great British institution, but it is no equivalent to the *Shabbat* meal, where prayers, biblical reminders and powerful symbols combine with a family meal to produce a profoundly spiritual event.

To give another example, at the festival of *Purim* it is

*Jewish Boy praying on the Mount of Olives*

traditional for a Jewish family to read the story of Esther at home in a dramatic and noisy way. All the children are given something to bang, shake or rattle. Whenever Haman, the villain of the piece, is mentioned they all hiss and make as much noise as possible; whenever Esther or her uncle Mordecai are named, they cheer. Far from turning this into a pantomime, the outcome is a gripping story in which even the youngest children become involved. Last year, when we did this as a family ourselves, the children cheered, banged their drums and stamped their feet at the appropriate moments with a rare exuberance. I am sure they will always remember the story. My joy at their involvement was tinged by the wish that my own Christian upbringing had included that sort of participation. (I still wonder what the neighbours made of it....)

Of course, most of the people who read this book or listen to the music of *City of Peace* will not be Jewish; neither will they live in Israel. But the point is that God knew how much help we need to live the life of faith. God knew that we need symbols, rituals and customs to help us understand profound spiritual truths: not because we're weak, or stupid, but because as human beings our senses of sight, hearing, touch, taste and smell are vital to our understanding and perception of the world in which we live. We are more than just a mind, and the life of God is to involve the whole person: that is why God's people were to talk about these things, not just in the synagogue but at home and as they walked down the road. These were words for the whole of life.

After the command to teach God's commandments to the next generation, come the commands to 'tie them as symbols on your hands and bind them on your foreheads; write them on the door-frames of your houses and on your gates. ' The first of these commands led to the wearing of *tefillin,* normally translated as phylacteries: these are worn by adult males at all weekday times of prayer. They consist of two small black boxes, each of which contains little scrolls of parchment upon which are written four passages from the *Torah,* the books of the Law. Attached to the boxes are leather straps, to tie them onto significant parts of the body. The first is bound onto the left arm, close to the heart, and thus to the seat of the emotions; it is symbolic of serving God with one's body. The leather strap (in Hebrew *retzuot*) is wound round the arm between the upper arm and the hand, the last portion being wrapped around the middle finger, as a reminder that Israel is the 'bride' of the Lord. Then the second box is placed on the forehead, the nearest point to the brain, the place of consciousness, thought and will; this symbolizes serving God with the intellect. Importantly, there is to be no interruption between putting on the first and second *tefillin,* to show that when it comes to serving God thought and action go together.

The second command led to the development of the *mezuzah,* the small parchment scroll contained in a case of wood, metal or (in recent years) plastic which is fixed to the doorpost of a house or a gateway. On the scroll are written two passages from Deuteronomy, the *Shema* and a call to obedience (Deut. 11. 13-21). When Jewish people go out through a door, enter their work-place, or go into a restaurant or hotel room, they touch the *mezuzah,* as a reminder of the omnipresence of God. The concept of 'practising the presence of God', made famous through Brother Lawrence's spiritual classic of that name, has become much more widely accepted within Christian circles in recent years. But think how much practising the presence there is in touching the *mezuzah.* It does not require a great effort of will or spiritual imagination;

it is just there, part of the everyday business of living. The physical habit leads to the 'earthing' of the spiritual truth that when I go out, I go in the name of God who is with me; and when I come back home, no matter where I've been or what my work has involved, the God who was with me at the outset is still with me on my return. This is very close to the understanding of Celtic spirituality.

There is a savage irony in the fact that the *tefillin* and *mezuzah* – the very things which God gave the Jewish people to keep them close to him and to strengthen their life of faith – have often been the focus for anti-Jewish sentiments during the Christian centuries, culminating in the Nazi propaganda during the Holocaust. There are still places where Jews are mocked and abused for wearing *tefillin,* in obedience to God's commandment to them.

I realize that many find these things difficult to apprehend. When we see a phylactery tied to the forehead of a Jewish man, or see a photograph of Jews praying at the Western Wall of the Temple in Jerusalem, a common Christian reaction is to find the symbols so alien that they make little sense to us. Perhaps some recoil from the thought that anyone might need special clothes or symbols to feel closer to God. Others may see only amazing faithfulness in God, a prayerful confidence that still causes this people, so many years on, to obey this command.

But think for a moment: the carpenter's house at Nazareth would have had a *mezuzah* on the door. The Jesus who said he had no intention of revoking one iota of the law (Matthew 5.17-18) must have worn *tefillin* himself as a God-fearing Jew. If he had not, it would have been a source of scandal and a guarantee that his message would not have been listened to at all.

What if we follow the example of Jesus – seen often in his teaching about the true application of the Law, and his desire

*The Wailing Wall*

to return to the original divine intention – and discover the underlying principle behind the God-given commandment. Can we imagine God saying to the Israelites, 'I am giving you a means by which you can know I am with you, know that I am your God and you are my people, every day of your lives'.

I sometimes wonder what would happen if, as Christians, we took the meaning of the *Shema* and its associated commandments more seriously. Would we discover a more incarnational – and a more human – way to keep in touch with God, precisely because of its combination of biblical text with physical and symbolic action? So many of us still limit ourselves to the written text alone, which is, of course, what God wanted his people to remember; but because of our wariness of symbols, gesture and movement in worship, we can so easily miss out on the wholesome and all-embracing ways God provided to let his word and the life of faith take root in the lives of his people.

What does alarm me is that these things which we Christians have jettisoned as being culturally conditioned, and therefore disposable, are the very things which God gave his people with a specific purpose in mind: to help them live in the knowledge that God the One Creator is their God, and that he is bound to them in covenant love.

# שְׁמַע יִשְׂרָאֵל יהוה אֱלֹהֵינוּ יהוה אֶחָד

*Shema Yisrael, Adonai Elohainu, Adonai Ehad.*
Hear, O Israel: The Lord our God, the Lord is One.

# For Reflection

## 1. When we recite the Shema

The six Hebrew words which constitute the *Shema* are the first words of prayer which we are called upon to teach our children. They are the last words to be uttered at life's end.

Each time we recite the *Shema*, we express our belief in the One, invisible, and incomparable God.

Each time we recite the *Shema*, we take upon ourselves the obligation to love Him with all our hearts, minds, and souls; to live faithfully by His commandments.

Each time we recite the *Shema*, we link ourselves to all the generations of Jews who steadfastly recited these sacred words; and we recall those who uttered those words as they prepared to surrender life itself rather than embrace an alien faith.

Each time we recite the *Shema*, we reaffirm that One God is the Parent of us all; and that all his children are related by a bond which transcends differences of origin or belief.

Each time we recite the *Shema*, we proclaim our creed, and hear a call for noble living in the presence of the Lord, our God.

From *Likrat Shabbath*, p.68

## 2. Listen!

Judaism begins with the commandment:
Hear, O Israel!
But what does it really mean to 'hear'?

The person who attends a concert
With a mind on business
Hears – but does not really hear.

The person who walks amid the songs of birds
And thinks only of what will be served for dinner
Hears – but does not really hear.

The man who listens to the words of his friend,
Or his wife, or his child,
And does not catch the note of urgency:
'Notice me, help me, care about me'
Hears – but does not really hear.

The person who listens to the news
And thinks only of how it will affect business
Hears – but does not really hear.

The person who stifles the sound of conscience
And thinks 'I have done enough already'
Hears – but does not really hear.

The person who hears the Hazzan pray
And does not feel the call to join in prayer
Hears – but does not really hear.

The person who listens to the rabbi's sermon
And thinks that someone else is being addressed
Hears – but does not really hear.

Today, O Lord,

Sharpen our ability to hear.

May we hear the music of the world,

And the infant's cry, and the lover's sigh.

May we hear the call for help of the lonely soul,

And the sound of the breaking heart.

May we also hear the words of our friends,

And also their unspoken pleas and dreams.

May we hear within ourselves the yearnings

That are struggling for expression.

May we hear You, O God.

For only if we hear You

Do we have the right to hope

That You will hear us.

Hear the prayers we offer to You this day, O God,

And may we hear them too.

Jack Riemer and Harold Kushner, adapted, from *Likrat Shabbat*, p. 74-75

# For Listening

## Shema (Hear, O Israel) - CD1

## City of Peace - CD1

Rabbi Hugo Gryn, a survivor of Auschwitz whose spiritual and ethical wisdom is widely known in the United Kingdom through his writings and radio broadcasts, has said, 'Zion is a kind of Jewish shorthand for the Kingdom of God found on earth'. The music of *City of Peace* begins with God's vision for his City of Peace, and the first section of the work reaches its climax with the first appearance of the title theme as an instrumental track. That choice was deliberate: we have much further to travel in this journey of faith before we dare translate God's sublime vision into words.

I wanted this music to combine the longing and the hope, the sorrow and the joy, the aspiration and the fulfilment, which are part of the final tapestry of Jerusalem, and to express something of the wonder of God's eternal purpose for this place, yet tinged by the sorrow and darkness of its history.

Earlier, I quoted some verses from the prophet Micah to show the essential meaning of 'shalom'. I should like to quote here the whole of the first part of that chapter, and to suggest that the reader might use it as a passage for meditation while listening to the instrumental version of *City of Peace*.

*In the last days, the mountain of the Lord's temple will be established as chief among the mountains; it will be raised above the hills, and peoples will stream to it. Many nations will come and say: 'Come, let us go up to the mountain of the Lord, to the house of the God of Jacob. He will teach us his ways so that we may walk in his paths.' The law will go out from Zion, the word of the Lord from Jerusalem. He will judge between many peoples and will settle disputes for strong nations far and wide. They will beat their swords into ploughshares and their spears into pruning hooks. Nation will not take up sword against nation, nor will they train for war any more. Every man will sit under his own vine and under his own fig tree, and no one will make them afraid, for the Lord Almighty has spoken.* (Micah 4. 1-4)

# chapter **five**

There is only one problem with a command like 'Hear, O Israel!' What happens if the people choose not to hear, choose neither to follow in his paths nor to obey his laws for life? I cannot begin to comprehend the sorrow in the heart of God whenever we ignore his initiatives to help us live in his love and peace.

Among the most catastrophic results of continuing human refusal to obey his laws for life is the shedding of innocent blood which began when Cain killed his brother. This provoked what is, for me, one of the most tragic cries in all Scripture:

*What have you done? Your brother's blood cries out to me from the ground. Now you are under a curse and driven from the ground, which opened its mouth to receive your brother's blood from your hand.*                                                        (Genesis 4.10)

How many times has God cried these words since the day of that murder when, for the first time in biblical history, the innocent blood of another human being is shed? But this cry from the heart of God takes us far beyond the story of Cain and Abel, into the daily suffering of men, women and children in the world of today. The ever- present, continually-updating news media have made us so familiar with the images of human suffering and slaughter, violence and genocide, that we can become hardened to what we see, hear and read, or even – God forgive us – bored when the same pictures of famine, massacre or homelessness come on the screens night after night.

*Yad Vashem, "Korczak and the Children of the Ghetto" by Boris Saktsier*

I want to suggest that another result of the media bombardment has been to dull our awareness of the cry of God. We have learned to become deaf to human pain and divine distress. Whether or not we are disturbed by the latest dreadful news from Bosnia, or Chechnya, or Rwanda, or wherever, we dare not forget that God still cries out in pain, suffering, every time one of his children is killed, maimed or abused or whenever a community is torn apart: 'What have you done? What have you done?'

The idea that God cries in pain, or indeed that God can suffer in any way, is a concept that appears only rarely in Christian theology from the days of the early Church Fathers to the nineteenth century. Suffering was something that came upon the individual or the community, but always against one's will. Suffering was inextricably associated with change, whether in the condition of society or an individual's physical well-being. Suffering was seen as a sign of weakness. To suffer pain was to be subject to something and, by definition, God could not be subject to anything. It followed that God had to be above suffering.

In the twentieth century theologians have come to see that such ideas fail to do justice to the God who revealed himself over many centuries through Scripture and in the life of his people. This God does get involved with his people, and goes on loving even those who, whether by their actions or by their indifference, spurn his love and spit in his face. Above all, this God reveals himself supremely in Jesus, the crucified God who died in physical pain and in the agony of separation from his eternal Father.

Suffering is not just something that God has heard about. The crucifixion is the sign that God knows suffering at first hand. God suffered on the cross, not because he had to but because he chose to.  Can we not also believe that God the Father also suffered in his love for his Son?

### 'Abraham, take your son'

It is only when I remember the suffering of God the Father in giving his Son to be crucified for the sins of the world, that I can approach one of the most moving narratives in the Jewish Bible.

Early on in the genesis of *City of Peace,* I realized that the story of Mount Moriah was going to be of central importance to the unfolding story of Jerusalem.  David is remembered as the great King and founder of Jerusalem, and at the time of writing Israel is celebrating the anniversary 3,000 years ago of the foundation of the city.  But Jewish people venerate Abraham as the Patriarch, the father of the nation to whom the great Covenant was given.

Mount Moriah is remembered by Jews as the traditional site of Abraham's near-sacrifice of his son Isaac.  This site has long been linked with the black rock at the top of the Temple Mount in Jerusalem, where Solomon built the first Temple. This is now contained within the Dome of the Rock, from where Muslims believe that the Prophet Mohammed ascended to heaven.  It is hard to imagine what the top of this venerated mountain would have looked like in Abraham's day, since for many centuries it has been covered by majestic buildings and surrounded by the Old City of Jerusalem.  What we can say is that on this place the hopes, fears, expectations and passionate devotion of Jews and Muslims have been focused in past centuries, and still co-exist and collide with inevitable consequences for the city and the world today.

Amongst the many glimpses into God's redeeming purposes found in the Jewish Bible – from the poetry of the

Psalms, the mystery surrounding Melchizedek, to the words of the Prophets, such as Isaiah's powerful portrayal of the Suffering Servant of God – the story of Abraham and Isaac is perhaps the most significant of all. Abraham, the man of faith, has already begun his journey into the unknown in obedience to the call of God.

*Some time later, God tested Abraham. He said to him, 'Abraham!'. 'Here I am,' he replied. Then God said, 'Take your son, your only son Isaac, whom you love, and go to the region of Moriah. Sacrifice him there as a burnt offering on one of the mountains I will tell you about.''*

(Genesis 22. 2)

These words never cease to move me. It is almost as if God was emphasising the pain that this awful demand would provoke. In fact, the words 'only son' would be better translated as 'favoured' or 'beloved' son. With each word, Isaac's uniqueness was being emphasised, and with it the immeasurable value that Abraham attached to him.

The rabbinic tradition understood there to have been ten tests or trials for Abraham, culminating in this climactic test on Moriah. For Abraham to become the founding father of Israel, he had to learn to give over his whole life, little by little, in trust to God. So when Abraham says 'here I am' in response to this command, it is the ultimate statement of obedience and faith.

Next morning Abraham, without any suggestion of argument (and this from the man who bargained with God over the fate of Sodom and Gomorrah), obeys and sets off with Isaac, two servants and sufficient wood for a burnt offering. Presumably he does this because, since God has once again not told him the final destination, Abraham cannot guarantee the availability of firewood at his journey's end. The effect, however,

*Difficult journey*

was that for the three days of the journey, the wood would be a constant reminder to Abraham of the horror which he was being asked to perform.

As a father, I can only begin to enter Abraham's heart and mind through the imagination, and try to picture his feelings and his fears as he set off with his son on the long climb to the top of Moriah, knowing all the time how it must end. He knew from the first step that the end of the journey he would either have to take his son's life or disobey the God who, against all hope and legitimate expectation, had promised the son in the first place. We can read the story with hindsight, knowing that all will be well in the end. But Abraham hadn't seen the last page of the script. How could Isaac be the son through whom the promised nation would arise, if he was now to be slaughtered? Were God's promises a delusion? Was Abraham's faithfulness a bitter lesson in futility?

After three days, Abraham and Isaac leave the servants behind and continue alone to face God on the mountain. And, at last, Isaac asks the inevitable question:

*'The fire and wood are here, but where is the lamb for the burnt offering?' Abraham answered, 'God himself will provide the lamb for the burnt offering, my son.'*

Abraham's answer should be read not as a bare-faced lie, but rather as a statement of faith in God. As we know, God's response to this awesome faithfulness was at the last moment, when Abraham had raised the knife to kill his beloved son, lying bound on the altar, to say: 'Stop, spare your son; look, here is a ram for the sacrifice'. I have been told that in Jewish folklore there is a version of this story told from the point of view of the ram! The innocent animal asks the question, 'Why me?'

In later years, Israel understood the principle that the first born belonged to God, but we sometimes forget that the Jewish people came to this understanding in the context of a world where child sacrifice was commonplace.

The idea of redemption through a surrogate sacrifice derives from this episode, where the founding father was directed by God to redeem his first-born son. In this respect Israel was unique amongst her neighbours. Here at Moriah we find not only the supreme test of Abraham's faith, but also a pre-echo of the passion of Jesus: the beloved son as sacrificial lamb; the submission of Isaac on Moriah and of Jesus in Gethsemane; the total faith of both Abraham and Jesus in their God. We need the story of Abraham and Isaac to understand what God the Father would do through his Son to redeem the world.

# For Reflection

## On a night of rain in Jerusalem

Some time ago I came across a remarkable poem by Uri Zvi Greenberg, one of the leading Jewish poets of the 20th century, which has brought me as much insight into the endlessness of Jerusalem's struggles and the meaning of Mount Moriah as any commentator, and which links the events of 3,500 years ago with Jerusalem of today.

*The few trees in the yard moan like a forest.*
*The thunderous clouds are heavy with rivers.*
*Angels of Peace stand at the head of my sleeping children,*
*As the trees moan and the heavy rains pour down.*

*Outside: Jerusalem, city of the Father's glorious trial,*
*Where he bound his son on one of the hills.*
*That fire, kindled at dawn, still burns on the hill,*
*The rains have not put it out:*
*It is the fire between the sacrificial pieces.*

*'If God were to command me now,*
*As once He did my ancient Father, I would surely obey'*
*Sing my heart and my flesh on this night of rain,*
*As the Angels of Peace stand at the head of my*
*sleeping children*
*What can equal this glory, this wondrous zeal -*
*Alive since that ancient dawn to this very moment -*

*Dark clouds over the mountains*

*for the Mount of Moriah?*
*The blood of the covenant sings on in the*
*Father's fervent body.*
*He is prepared to offer his sacrifice on the*
*Temple Mount at dawn.*

*Outside: Jerusalem and the moaning of the Lord's trees,*
*Cut down by her enemies in every generation;*
*Clouds are heavy with rain, lightnings in them and thunders*
*Which, for me, in this night of rain,*
*Are tidings from the mouth of the God of might*
*To endless generations.*

based on a poem by Uri Zvi Greenberg b. 1896, from *The Penguin Book of Hebrew Verses*

For Jewish people, Mount Moriah remains as a timeless symbol of their father Abraham's willingness to sacrifice his son. Only on Mount Moriah, the place of God's choosing, could the permanent central sanctuary of the Jewish people be built. *On a night of rain in Jerusalem* points to the significance of that story and that sanctuary to endless generations.

Some of the expressions used by Uri Zvi Greenberg are steeped in Old Testament imagery. 'That fire, kindled at dawn' refers to the fire which was kindled for the sacrifice. It may also be a symbol of Abraham's faith, which still burns brightly at the Western Wall of the Temple, where Jews from around the world offer prayer to the God of Abraham, Isaac and Jacob. The 'fire between the sacrificial pieces' goes back to Genesis 15.9-18:

*The Lord said to him, 'Bring me a heifer, a goat and a ram, each three years old, along with a dove and a young pigeon.' Abram brought all these to him, cut them in two and arranged the halves opposite each other; the birds, however, he did not cut in half....As the sun was setting, Abram fell into a deep sleep, and a thick and dreadful darkness came over him....When the sun had set and darkness had fallen, a smoking fire pot with a blazing torch appeared and passed between the pieces. On this day, God made a covenant with Abram.*

Another expression which may need some explanation is 'the Lord's trees'. While this could be taken to refer to the trees of a forest, in the Old Testament the words 'the trees of the Lord' are also used to symbolize the people of God. For example, Isaiah writes,

*They will be called oaks of righteousness, a planting of the Lord for the display of his splendour.*                    (Isaiah 61. 3b)

I have come to recognise that Messianic Jews, and particularly those who live in and around Jerusalem, or those from further afield who know their history and their heritage, are specially placed to teach us the meaning and the sense of all this. Uniquely, they can understand the significance of this tiny little piece of land which Abraham knew as Mount Moriah, which Solomon knew as the Temple Mount, and where Jesus taught about himself and about the Kingdom of God.

Across the Valley to the East is the Mount of Olives; to the South, Mount Zion, the original city founded by David; and all around, the Old City of Jerusalem, outside whose walls stood Golgotha, the quarry which doubled as the municipal execution site. Each site within sight of each other; and all within minutes of the place where Abraham and Isaac provided the prototype for the willingness of a loving father to sacrifice his son.

Messianic Jews are also uniquely placed to understand the turbulence of this holy site, a turbulence which Uri Zvi Greenberg clearly believes will endure 'through endless generations'. For Christians, there are also tremendous resonances here with the turbulence described in the gospel accounts of the sacrifice of Jesus, with the darkness, the thunder and lightning of the crucifixion narratives.

## For Listening

### The Cry and Night 2 CD 2
In *The Cry* we hear God's endless cry over the pain and suffering in his world. The dark, troubled music of *Night 2*, the instrumental piece which follows, is intended to convey something of the consequences of the human capacity for shedding of innocent blood.

### Moriah CD1
In writing this song, I followed closely the account in Genesis 22.

*Avraham, Avraham –*
*Take your son, your only son,*
*beloved one, to the land of Moriah.*
*Prepare the wood for a sacrifice*
*and carry with you fire and knife.*

On the horizon, where the mountain stands,
bring your son, build an altar with your hands,
then bind him with cords and cover his eyes
upon the stones set Isaac down to lie.

O my father –
Behold the wood and the fire and the knife,
but where is the lamb for the sacrifice?
We have travelled far and I long for home
and soon the light of day will be gone.

God will provide Himself the lamb –
I do not fully understand,
but I trust him still in life, in death,
through him I breathe my every breath,
my son.

Do you love me?
You know that I do.
Avraham, Avraham –
Lay not your hand on him, nor wound him,
for now I know you fear me, love me more than all.
Because of this indeed I bless you,
because you answered when I called.

*And as the stars that dwell in the heavens*

*And grains of sand upon the shore,*

*So shall be your children and your children's children.*

*My words shall stand for evermore*

*and all nations of the earth shall prosper*

*because your faith in me stood firm,*

*when I dared to ask of you the sacrifice*

*of your beloved only son.*

based on Genesis 22

With *Moriah* there begins what is in effect a Passion sequence within *City of Peace*. It begins when the choir sings 'Behold the wood and the fire and the knife', words first spoken by Isaac. The sound picture was built up during the recording session by combining several different ways of articulating the words. Some of the choir sing them, others hum, others whisper, trying to imagine their own terror as they witness the climactic moments in the sequence of events which led to Jesus' death. The intention was to create a sense of the chaos and confusion and fear surrounding the events of betrayal, arrest and trial.

Abraham passes the test. This last stanza of *Moriah* is a paraphrase of the words of the angel, who now restates, for the seventh and last time, the great promises of God to Abraham in their most generous form (Genesis 22.15-18).

## On a Night of Rain in Jerusalem and Night CD1

I try to convey something of Jerusalem's turbulence in *Night*, the instrumental movement which follows *On a Night of Rain in Jerusalem*.

# chapter **six**

As I wrote at the outset, this book is not so much a history of Jerusalem – there are already plenty of good histories available – as one man's reflections on the meaning and mystery of this city. Nearly 2,000 years elapsed between Abraham's offering on Mount Moriah and the coming of Yeshua, but from that rich tapestry of Jerusalem's story I propose to pick out only three threads.

## Exile

The first is exile. It is impossible to over-estimate the significance to Jewish thought and spirituality down the centuries of the fall of Judah to Nebuchadnezzar in 597 and the final capture of Jerusalem in 586, when the city walls were destroyed and Solomon's temple and palace were razed to the ground. Historians dispute exactly how many people were taken off into exile in Babylon, but it is clear that amongst the exiles were all the leaders of the religious, political and economic life of Judaic society.

The dynasty of David, which had ruled in Jerusalem for around 400 years, had come to an end. Though David's line became increasingly associated with God's future salvation of his people, the downfall of the Davidic king and loss of national integrity meant that the people's sense of identity had now to be focused on their religion.

Even here there was little comfort. For the exiles and for those who remained behind in Judaea as an impoverished remnant, the questions and the doubts persisted. The prophets had told them repeatedly that their continuing rebellion against God would have catastrophic consequences: had God now abandoned them, or failed them? Was their God powerless in the face of the gods of Babylon? Was God's Covenant with the children of Abraham now at an end? Was there any way back into his favour and his love?

For those who were deported the situation was particularly acute, despite the sense of solidarity they developed as a community of exiles in Babylon. For them, as for all Jews in exile, separation from Jerusalem was virtually tantamount to separation from God. Even as they were working out a means of worshipping God without the familiar pattern of Temple worship and sacrifice, they knew something was missing. It was at this time that the return to Zion and the restoration and rebuilding of Jerusalem assumed their central place within Jewish worship.

Although it was written roughly mid-way through the later, longer exile between the destruction of Jerusalem in A.D. 70 by the Romans and the foundation of the state of Israel, this poem *To Israel in Exile* conveys powerfully many of the themes of the earlier exile in Babylon.

*O sleeper, whose heart is awake, burning and raging,*
*now wake and go forth, and walk in the light of my presence.*

*Rise and ride on! A star has come forth for you,*
*and he who has lain in the pit will go up to the top of*

אתר זה מנציח אלפי קהילות ישראל

שחו תחת שלטון גרמניה הנאצית וגרורותיה.
רובן המכריע חרבו בשואה. מיעוטן שרדו אך נפגעו קשות

למעלה מאלף שנים ישבו היהודים על אדמת אירופה,
בנו את קהילותיהם ושמרו על ייחודם הלאומי והדתי.
הם ידעו ימים של שקט ופריחה תרבותית,
וימי שפל שבהם נאלצו ליטול את מקל וינדודים.
לחפש מקומות חדשים ולשקם את קהילותיהם
בכל מקום בו ישבו תרמו מכישרונם לעמים שבקרבם חיו

בבקעה זו יישמר זכרם לעד.

THIS MEMORIAL COMMEMORATES THE JEWISH COMMUNITIES DESTROYED
BY NAZI GERMANY AND ITS COLLABORATORS AND THE FEW WHICH SURVIVED
BUT SURVIVED IN THE SHADOW OF THE HOLOCAUST

FOR MORE THAN A THOUSAND YEARS JEWS LIVED IN EUROPE, ORGANIZING
COMMUNITIES PRESERVING THEIR DISTINCT IDENTITY
IN PERIODS OF RELATIVE TRANQUILITY JEWISH CULTURE FLOURISHED
BUT IN PERIODS OF UNREST JEWS WERE FORCED TO FLEE
WHEREVER THEY SETTLED, THEY ENDOWED
THE PEOPLE AMONGST WHOM THEY LIVED WITH THEIR TALENTS

AND THEIR STORIES WILL BE TOLD

*'... In periods of relative tranquility Jewish culture flourished, but in periods of unrest Jews were forced to flee...' Memorial plaque at Yad Vashem.*

*Sinai. Let them not exult, those who say 'Zion is*
*desolate!' – for my heart is in Zion, and my eyes are there.*

*I reveal myself and I conceal myself,*
*now I rage, now I consent –*
*but who has more compassion than I have for my children.*

by Judah Halevi (c.1100), from *The Penguin Book of Hebrew Verse*

Judah Halevi was a Spanish Jew at a time when Christians and Muslims fought over Spain, with catastrophic results for the Jewish community. Halevi's personal experiences of persecution led him to consider the meaning of exile – what it meant to be a Jew of the Diaspora – and this led to his decision at the end of his life to emigrate to the Holy Land. According to Professor Ted Carmi, 'no Hebrew poet since the Psalmists had sung the praise of the Holy Land with such passion... the longing for Zion, the pain of parting from his cultural environment.'

Apart from the longing for Jerusalem, this poem also has within it not only the explicit declaration of God's enduring compassion for his people, but also the implicit sense of the people's longing for Messiah to come. There is also more than a hint that God has been watching and waiting for the right moment to end the pain of exile. The statement that 'my heart is in Zion' contains the reassurance that he has not abandoned his people, nor removed himself from his holy city, in itself a profound guarantee that one day the desolation of Zion will be at an end, and the exiles will return.

Given that background, the phrase 'I reveal myself and I conceal myself' begins to take on deeper meaning. God seems to make himself present by the sense of his absence; almost as if God were in hiding, but yet drawing his people to him in truer discipleship, as they sought him in the unknown. There are also resonances in Halevi's poem with the Exodus from Egypt. Just as God led the Israelites out of Egypt by a column of fire or of cloud, so the returning exiles were to 'walk in the light of my presence.'

## Repentance and Return

One of the reasons the experience of exile was so devastating for the Jews was because of the former intimacy of their relationship with God. The pattern of relationship which emerges from the Old Testament can be described as a cycle of rebellion, repentance and return. The people grow complacent, forget God and ignore his laws for life. God continues to demonstrate his love for them until they repent, and return into his favour. While the prophets rammed home the solemn warnings and called for repentance, yet they also reminded the people that it was God's nature 'always to have mercy'.

One prophetic passage which combines the above in a single span is Hosea chapter 11. We read of God's nurture of the infant Israel, of the people's idolatry and sin, their refusal to return to him, of the consequences of that rebellion. And we read also of the dilemma in the heart of God, the dilemma of a God of justice who cannot bring himself to abandon the people he loves. Though Hosea was speaking to Jews, his analysis is true for all humanity. These are ways in which 'all have sinned, and fallen short of the glory of God' (Romans 3.23).

*When Israel was a child, I loved him, and out of Egypt I called my son. But the more I called Israel, the further they went from me. They sacrificed to the Baals and they burned incense to images. It was I who taught Ephraim to walk, taking them by the arms; but they did not realise it was I who healed them. I led them with cords of human kindness, with ties of love; I lifted the yoke from their neck and bent down to feed them.*

*Will they not return to Egypt and will not Assyria rule over them because they refuse to repent? Swords will flash in their cities, will destroy their gates and put an end to their plans. My people are determined to turn from me. Even if they call to the Most High, he will by no means exalt them.*

*How can I give you up, Ephraim? How can I hand you over, Israel? How can I treat you like Admah? How can I make you like Zeboiim? My heart is changed within me; all my compassion is aroused. I will not carry out my fierce anger, not devastate Ephraim again. For I am God, and not man – the Holy One among you. I will not come in wrath.*                                              (Hosea 11. 1-9)

These verses were the original inspiration behind *My every breath,* a song in which I wanted to develop in poetry and music the prophet's image of a human father and child as a metaphor for the intimate relationship between God and his people Israel.

> *I would never ever leave you*
> *I watched over your first footsteps*
> *Come to me and I will give you rest*

*Ever since you were a child,*
*I loved you as a father loves his own.*
*But the more I sought to bring you home*
*The more you wandered far away*

*How you strained to break away alone*
*With hardened eyes*
*How you turned your open hearts*
*to hearts of stone*
*We could have made this journey hand in hand*
*Enjoyed the goodness of this land... couldn't we?*

*Now a darkness falls upon you*
*Blinds your eyes and turns your gold to dust.*
*But my heart is changed within me,*
*How compassion fills my every breath.*

based on Hosea 11

This is the familiar, touching picture of a father and child walking hand in hand, seen in any city street or park. It reminds me of the days when my own children were in their infancy. Yet just as any little child will from time to time try to escape parental control, and with it the security provided by a caring parent, so time and again the people of the Covenant 'strained to break away alone' from their Father God, with disastrous results at both national and personal level.

*Security*

Despite this, the mood of this text is not laboured or dark, but rather a mixture of sadness and hope. The reason for the optimism is found in the final words: 'How compassion fills my every breath'. Our ground for hope is the love of God which, despite repeated rebellion, refused to give up on the people he had chosen: 'How can I give you up, Ephraim? How can I hand you over, Israel?' (Hosea 11.8a).

In writing this song I thought a great deal about the word 'breath' and its importance within a number of biblical passages. It appears in the Genesis account of the creation, as God breathed life into Adam (Genesis 2.7); and in Ezekiel's vision of the dry bones, where the fully-fleshed bodies still require breath in order to come alive:

*Then he said to me, 'Prophesy to the breath; prophesy, son of man, and say to it, "This is what the Sovereign Lord says: Come from the four winds, O breath, and breathe into these slain, that they may live."' So I prophesied as he commanded me, and breath entered them; they came to life and stood up on their feet, a vast army.*

(Ezekiel 37.9-10)

All this speaks to me of God's involvement in his creation in a way which is at once both infinite and powerful. The essence of Ezekiel's vision is that a body without breath is no more than an assemblage of flesh and bones – an empty shell. Only when God gives the breath of life do we come into being, and personality and individuality begin to emerge. Our every breath is the result of his initial gift of life and his continuing sustaining of life. We are utterly dependent on him every moment of our existence. The fact that both in Hebrew and Greek the word for breath *(ruach* and *pneuma* respectively) can mean spirit or wind, only serves to reinforce the point.

As we know, human frailty and rebellion frustrate the divine purpose, at least for a while. It is almost as if each of us can only be breathed along a certain distance at a time, just as a child's sailing boat needs many puffs of wind to cross the pool. Therefore, while the tone of this song is generally hopeful, there remains a wistful sadness :

*How you strained to break away alone, with hardened eyes*

*How you turned your open hearts to hearts of stone*

*We could have made this journey hand in hand*

*Enjoyed the goodness of this land...couldn't we?*

In an Advent sermon broadcast on BBC1 a few years ago, Fr Herbert McCabe O.P. said: 'Nothing can drag me back to the land of shadows, but I could, if I really work at it, make my way back myself'. Cutting loose from God is hard work, and the struggle of our flight from perfect love often – perhaps always – results in a hardness in our eyes which mirrors an inner hardness of soul. Hearts which were created to be open to God turn into hearts of stone, the reverse of that other powerful image found in Ezekiel:

*For I will take you out of the nations; I will gather you from all the countries and bring you back into your own land. I will sprinkle clean water on you, and you will be clean. I will cleanse you from all your impurities and from all your idols. I will give you a new heart and put a new spirit in you. I will give you a new heart and give you a heart of flesh. And I will put my Spirit in you and move you to follow my decrees and be careful to keep my laws.* (Ezekiel 36.24-27)

The compassionate God will always have the last word. For his every breath, every movement of the Spirit, is filled with his love and compassion, and his desire to bring us home.


## Day of Atonement

It was perhaps inevitable that national and personal repentance should become focused on a specific religious festival. This was the Day of Atonement (in Hebrew, *Yom Kippur*), the solemn day of repentance and fasting which comes ten days after *Rosh Hashanah*, the Jewish New Year.

*Yom Kippur* is one of the greatest festivals of Judaism, and is sometimes called the *Shabbat Shabbaton*, the Sabbath of Sabbaths. Its detailed and symbol-laden ritual is described in Leviticus chapter 16. It was at *Yom Kippur* that the High Priest went into the Holy of Holies in the temple, and sprinkled the blood of a bull for his own sins, and of a goat to make atonement for all the sin and uncleanness of the people of Israel. The other goat required for the ritual became the scapegoat, a word and a concept which has passed into many cultures. The scapegoat, after being presented alive to the Lord, was carried to the outskirts of the community, where it was released into the desert, 'burdened' with the sins of the people which it then carried away.

*He is to lay both hands on the head of the live goat and confess over it all the wickedness and rebellion of the Israelites – all their sins – and put them on the goat's head. He shall send the goat away into the desert in the care of a man appointed for the task. The goat will carry on itself all their sins to a solitary place; and the man shall release it in the desert.* (Leviticus 16.20-22)

*Yom Kippur* is central to the Jewish understanding of forgiveness and reconciliation with God and neighbour. *Yom Kippur* was the time of repentance and confession. Since there was no atonement for sins committed against one's neighbour unless the neighbour had first agreed to forgive the offence, the days between *Rosh Hashanah* and *Yom Kippur* were also days of reconciliation, when people sought out those they had grieved in any way.

The atmosphere within Jewish communities throughout the world changes at the time of *Yom Kippur;* even the increasingly secular society of contemporary Israel keeps this as a national day of repentance. There is much deep emotion in Jerusalem, as the Chief Rabbis pronounce prayers of repentance for the nation and for all Israel's failure and sin. It was because Israel was concentrating on the religious festival on this most holy of days that the Arab states launched the 1967 war on that day: in human terms, a brilliant military strategy; in another sense, an unspeakable blasphemy. As we shall see, for the first Christians *Yom Kippur* provided an important part of the framework within which they began to understand the meaning of Jesus' death.

# For Reflection

## 'Ride on, O Lord our warrior, and lead your people home'

These words are the starting point for *Lion of Judah*, which combines the themes of exile, repentance and return with the growing expectancy that God would send the Messiah to bring his people home. This piece is also based on a prophecy of Hosea.

*Come, let us return unto the Lord our God;*
*he has torn us into pieces,*
*but he will heal us.*

*Let us set ourselves to follow him in all his ways,*
*for he caused our feet to stumble;*
*with humble hearts we come.*

*His presence will enfold us, he will bind our wounds;*
*for we know he will revive us,*
*after three days he shall raise us.*

*He will appear as surely as the rising sun;*
*he will come to us like the winter rains,*
*for his ways are right and we shall walk in them.*
*Let the desert and the cities raise their voices high;*
*let the people shout from the mountain tops,*

*let the stones cry out – for he is King.*
*Hope is with the hopeless and our fears are gone.*
*Ride on, O Lord, our warrior,*
*and lead your people home.*

*Lion of Judah, rock of ages,*
*so revealed through endless pages.*
*Prince of Peace to every nation;*
*surely God is my salvation.*

*You will lead us, we shall follow;*
*no more darkness, no more sorrow.*
*Did our hearts not burn within us,*
*As his words were opened to us?*

*We are ransomed, healed, forgiven;*
*it is true, the Lord is risen.*
*Satan's power for ever broken,*
*Heaven's gates for ever open.*

based on Hosea 6

In performance I often talk to the audience about the names and titles ascribed to Jesus throughout Scripture, as a way of understanding his ministry and the meaning of his death and resurrection. For this reason, I wanted to fill the chorus of *Lion of Judah* with phrases which describe the Messiah, his power, his authority and the result of his ministry.

The first hint of 'Lion of Judah' is in Genesis 49.9, but the full ascription of this title to Jesus comes in Revelation 5.5: 'Do not weep! See, the Lion of Judah, the Root of David, has triumphed'. 'Rock of ages', made famous by Toplady's hymn, derives from the incident in Exodus 17.6, where Moses struck the rock at Horeb and water gushed out from the people to drink. St Paul makes the connection with Jesus: 'Also they all ate the same food from the Spirit and they all drank the same drink from the Spirit – for they drank from a Spirit-sent Rock which followed them, and that Rock was the Messiah' (1 Corinthians 10.3-4, taken from *Jewish New Testament*, a recent translation from the Greek by Dr David H. Stern, a Messianic Jew). 'Prince of Peace' comes from the great Messianic prophecy in Isaiah 9: 'And he will be called Wonderful Counsellor, Mighty God, Everlasting Father, Prince of Peace'. 'Surely God is my salvation' is closely linked with his name, Yeshua, which means 'Yahweh saves'.

While it was important to represent the names and titles of Old Testament prophecy, I wanted also to include in this song events found in the New Testament. So amidst the prophetic titles there are also clear references to the risen *Yeshua*, his walk with the two downcast disciples on the road to Emmaus, the promise of the Kingdom found in Revelation 21. 4 – 'He will wipe every tear from their eyes' – and to the final victory over Satan and all the powers of evil.

For it is on account of the ministry of Jesus, from creation to redemption, that we can have confidence to turn to him and, through him, to return to our Father God. This desire to repent and return, both individually and as a community, is at the heart of *Lion of Judah*.

# For Listening

### To Israel in Exile CD2

### My Every Breath CD2

### Day of Atonement/Lamb of God CD1

In the instrumental section at the beginning of this track I wanted to convey something of the darkness and turbulence of that public consciousness and confession of sin.

### Lion of Judah CD2

# chapter **seven**

*In the past God spoke to our forefathers through the prophets at many times and in various ways, but in these last days he has spoken to us by his Son, whom he appointed heir of all things, and through whom he made the universe. The Son is the radiance of God's glory and the exact representation of his being, sustaining all things by his powerful word. After he had provided purification for sins, he sat down at the right hand of the Majesty in heaven.* (Hebrews 1. 1-3)

If Christians are ever tempted to assume that Jesus was born in some kind of religious or cultural limbo, unexpected and unlooked for, then these few short verses should be enough to dispel those assumptions for good. The unknown author of the letter to the Hebrews – or 'to a group of Messianic Jews', as the Epistle is described in the *Jewish New Testament* translation – reminds his readers at the outset of the cosmic significance of the man Yeshua they worship as Lord. He writes of his role in the creation of the world and in the sustaining of the created order, of the incarnation in a Bethlehem stable of 'the radiance of the *Sh'khinah*, the very expression of God's essence' (Hebrews 1.3, *Jewish New Testament*), of his death and resurrection, and his ascension to the right hand of God.

Dr Walter Riggans, in his fascinating book *Jesus Ben Joseph*, writes: '*[It is not] a mere accident that the incarnate Son of God became a Jewish man in the land known by the Romans as Palestine. Only the Jewish people had been given promises of the coming of this Messiah; only they were expecting him and praying for his coming.*'

From *Jesus Ben Joseph*, published by Monarch 1993

We often forget this. Anyone who goes to a Christmas carol service is bound to hear the prologue to St John's gospel: 'He was in the world, and though the world was made through him, the world did not recognise him. He came to that which was his own, but his own did not receive him'. The coming of Messiah was both looked for and prayed for. The twelfth of the 'Thirteen Principles of Faith' in the Jewish Prayer Book, the *Siddur* says this: "I believe with perfect faith in the coming of the Messiah, and, though he tarry, I wait daily for his coming.' The Messiah appeared time and again in the words of the Old Testament prophets, from the Suffering Servant of Isaiah 53 (which Jewish scholars from the Babylonian *Talmud* until mediaeval times saw as a Messianic prophecy) to the Son of Man described in Daniel 7. 1-28.

Even the Messiah's birthplace was anticipated. The first mention of Bethlehem as the birthplace of David comes in 1 Samuel 16.1, where the prophet is sent by God to anoint a new King as successor to the rejected Saul:

*Fill your horne with oil and be on your way; I am sending you to Jesse of Bethlehem. I have chosen one of his sons to be King.*

Micah mentions Bethlehem in the context of messianic prophecy:

*But you, Bethlehem Ephratha, though you are small among the clans of Judah, out of you will come for me one who will be ruler over the Israel, whose origins are from of old, from ancient times.* (Micah 5.2)

This last prophecy is acknowledged as Messianic in the *Targum Jonathan,* an authoritative text written in the second century of the Christian era.

Jewish apocalyptic literature, most of which was written in the two centuries before the birth of Jesus and the first century of the Christian era, concentrated even more closely on the coming of the Messiah, with the result that Jewish understanding of who Messiah was and what he would do took on a more precise form during this period. According to the Jewish Encyclopedia, 'the title "Messiah" as a designation of the eschatological personality does not exist in the Old Testament; it occurs only from the time of the Second Temple after the Old Testament period....In Rabbinic thought, the Messiah is the king who will redeem and rule Israel at the climax of human history and the instrument by which the kingdom of God will be established' (*Encyclopedia Judaica*, p. 1408; Kefer Publishing House, Jerusalem 1972).

The debate about the identity and nature of the Messiah continues to the present day. In his book *To Be A Jew*, Rabbi Hayim Halevy Donin writes:

*The Messiah in Jewish thought was never conceived of as a Divine Being. As God's anointed representative, the Messiah would be a person who would bring about the political and spiritual redemption of the people Israel through the ingathering of the Jews to their ancestral home of Eretz Yisrael and the restoration of Jerusalem to its spiritual glory. He would bring about an era marked by the perfection of all mankind and the harmonious co-existence of all peoples free of war, fear, hatred and intolerance. Claimants to the Messianic title arose at various times throughout Jewish history. The criterion by which each was judged was: Did he succeed in accomplishing what the Messiah was supposed to accomplish? By this criterion, clearly none qualified.*

Rabbi Hayim Halevy Donin, from *To Be A Jew,* p. 15

As a Christian, I cannot accept Rabbi Donin's conclusions; he would not expect me to. But what is clear is that the birth of Jesus came after centuries of expectation of the Messiah, and of countless years study of the texts which spoke of his coming.

On the day that the baby Yeshua was brought by his parents to be dedicated to God, there were two people present in the Temple who had been praying for the coming of Messiah. The first was a priest called Simeon (in Hebrew, Shim'on) to whom it had been revealed that he would not die until he had seen the Messiah.

*Prompted by the Spirit, he went into the Temple courts; and when the parents brought in the child Jesus to do for him what the Torah required, Shim'on took him in his arms, made a b'rakhah [praise] to God, and said: 'Now, Adonai, according to your word, your servant is at peace as you let him go; for I have seen with my own eyes your Yeshu'ah, which you prepared in the presence of all peoples – a light that will bring revelation to the Goyim [gentiles] and glory to your people Israel'.* (Luke 2.27-32, *Jewish New Testament*)

The other was Anna, an elderly prophetess:

*She was very old; she had lived with her husband seven years after her marriage, and then was a widow until she was eighty-four. She never left the temple, but worshipped night and day, fasting and praying. Coming up to them at that very moment, she gave thanks to God and spoke about the child to all who were looking forward to the redemption of Jerusalem.* (Luke 2.36-38)

•••••

Walter Riggans goes on to write,

*Jesus' Jewishness was part of him; it deeply influenced him; it helped to define him. And let us not forget that it defined the disciples and everyone else around him.*

It was only when I visited Israel that the truth of this struck me forcibly, and I came to realize that I had never really come to terms with the full meaning of Jesus' Jewishness. Intellectually, of course, I could accept that as fact, but the concept of a Jewish Jesus did not fit with the range of imagery and ways of thinking about Jesus that I had inherited. Not that I am alone in this. Many Christians have problems in accepting this notion of Jesus the Jew, whether as a result of residual (and sometimes not so residual) anti-semitism or because the Church, for obvious reasons, has tended to emphasise the *differences* between Christianity and Judaism, rather than the continuities and points of shared understanding.

For Jews, the difficulty in accepting the Jewishness of Jesus is even greater. The effect of anti-semitism and the long history of persecution visited on them by those who call themselves Christians –- pogroms, persecutions, enforced segregation in ghettoes, down to the abyss of the Holocaust – has been to make it near-impossible for Jewish people to see Jesus as Jewish until relatively resently. Given the fact that even in his own day Jesus was not really 'one of us', it is not surprising that from early on there developed a propaganda which portrayed Jesus as a renegade, not really Jewish at all – by birth, perhaps, but not by behaviour.

For St Matthew, whose gospel is the other New Testament book which speaks most directly to Christians from a Jewish background, Jesus' Jewish lineage is so important that he begins his gospel with a detailed genealogy. Reading this genealogy in a translation which gives the characters their authentic Jewish names brings that context to life in a new way

*This is the genealogy of Yeshua the Messiah, son of David, son of Avraham....* (Matthew 1.1, *Jewish New Testament*)

Although it makes for rather turgid reading in a liturgical setting, and is almost guaranteed to dissuade the uncommitted private reader from further investigation, this genealogy is fascinating for the way it places Jesus in the context of his family heritage and national history. The nation into whose royal line Jesus was born characterized themselves above all as 'people of the Torah', contained in the Five Books of Moses whose interpretation continues to dominate Rabbinical studies. Jesus took the Torah so seriously that he said 'Do not think I have come to abolish the Law and the prophets; I have come not to abolish them, but to fulfil them' (Matt 5:17). The Law governed everything. According to the Torah, the Virgin Mary could have been stoned to death for being pregnant before marriage. Seen in this light, Joseph's decision to divorce her quietly, not only to avoid scandal but for her protection and survival, takes on new meaning.

In accordance with the Torah, and in common with all Jewish male infants, Yeshua was circumcised on the 8th day. Just as he wore phylacteries, the external symbols of the Covenant, so he bore in his body the sign and symbol of the Covenant. As Jesus grew up, the clothes he wore were made in accordance with Jewish law and practice, with no mixing of fibres within one garment. In obedience to the Torah, the corners of those clothes would have been edged with tassels (in Hebrew *tzitzit*, and translated in the Authorized Version as 'fringes'), as a visual reminder of God's commandments and the people's responsibility to live them. It was this 'fringe of his garment' that was touched by the woman with the twelve year haemorrhage, leading to her healing (Matthew 9:20-21).

Although the gospels record Jesus throwing new light on the (then) traditional interpretation of the regulations governing Shabbat, nowhere do the gospels suggest Jesus broke the dietary laws. If he had, why should it still have been such a major problem for Peter when, in his vision in Acts 10, he is told to eat unclean animals? It remained a massive spiritual and psychological hurdle for Peter because he had never seen Jesus eat unclean foods.

Jesus was born into a society whose life was attuned to the rhythm of worship. So we read that 'he went to the synagogue, as his custom was, on the Sabbath' (Luke 4:16-30), where the emphasis was on the reading of scripture, its exposition and daily prayer. For the major religious festivals of Judaism, however, the God-fearing Jew would turn to the Temple in Jerusalem. Jesus was first brought to the temple as a baby, when he was recognised by Simeon and Anna. That same chapter of Luke's gospel records that Jesus' parents went to Jerusalem for the Feast of the Passover every year. It was while on the way home from one of these annual visits that Jesus could not be found, until his parents went back to Jerusalem and discovered him deep in debate with the rabbis in the temple courts (Luke 2:41-52), not far from the place where the daily round of sacrifices were offered.

Jesus' visits to Jerusalem at major festivals became focal points in his public ministry, not least because he was unafraid to apply the Messianic references of these festivals and their rituals to himself, despite the controversy that provoked. For example, the Feast of Tabernacles (in Hebrew, *Sukkot*)

*Jews praying and reading the scriptures at the Wailing Wall*

*Celebration meal*

celebrates the gathering of the crops from the fields but also a deeper remembrance of the huts in which the Israelites lived during their years of wandering in the wilderness. The emphasis is on the people's dependence on God and on God's faithfulness to his people. The fact that Tabernacles came at the end of a hot, dry summer, meant that prayers for the Autumn rains were incorporated into the ritual. In trust that God would provide rains, a large golden pitcher of water from the pool of Siloam was poured out. It was at Tabernacles that Jesus said 'If anyone is thirsty, let him come to me and drink'. Another symbol at this festival was light: the Court of the Women in the Temple was lit by 400 lamps set on high columns, which were said to illuminate all the homes of Jerusalem. It was at the Feast of Tabernacles that Jesus said 'I am the Light of the World'.

If the symbolism of Tabernacles was used by Jesus to illustrate his identity and his mission, it was the Feast of Passover (*Pesach*) which above all enabled his disciples to understand the meaning and significance of his crucifixion. At Pesach the Jewish people celebrate their salvation from slavery in Egypt and how God made them into a nation in Covenant with himself, a God who keeps his promises and delivers his people Israel from oppression. It would have been taken for granted that Jesus would keep the Passover. The issue was where – not whether – Jesus and his disciples would share the Passover meal.

Jesus came to Jerusalem at Passover to die. The symbolism of that first Holy Week means so much more when we understand more fully the meaning of Passover. Bread and wine, for example, were integral parts of the ritual Passover meal. The piece of unleavened bread (*afikomen*) which was broken off symbolised the Passover lamb, and was eaten after the meal so that the final taste was a reminder of the sacrifice which made salvation possible. In the Passover meal were four 'drinkings' of wine. The third of these was the Cup of Redemption. This came just after the meal, as the gospels indicate, and was used by Jesus to point to the redemption won through the shedding of his blood.

The first disciples, all of them Jews, came to see that on the cross Jesus combined the meaning of Passover and Yom Kippur, uniting salvation and liberation with atonement for sin. They knew he had been arrested on the eve of Passover. They worshipped him as the Passover Lamb of God, whose innocent blood was shed for the sins of the people, and whose death ensured that all who believe in him would 'pass over' from death to life. Golgotha pointed them to the scapegoat theology of Yom Kippur. They understood Jesus as the incarnate 'scapegoat' , who was taken outside the city walls bearing the sins of the people, and crucified to make 'purification for sins' – the fulfilment of the sacrificial system, and its end.

# For Reflection

In St John's account of Jesus' resurrection appearance to the disciples by the lakeside (John 21.15-17), the risen Jesus three times asks Peter this simple question:

*'Do you love me?'*

I remember hearing a sermon, when I was still a teenager, where the preacher made a great impact on me. He said that St John's account of this breakfast by the lakeside is one of only two places that the word for charcoal is used in the gospels: the other is in John 18.18, where Peter warmed his hands in the courtyard outside the High Priest's house. Three times Peter denied his Lord beside a charcoal fire; three times, by a different charcoal fire, the risen Jesus gives him an opportunity to wipe out that denial. Bishop Lesslie Newbigin offers a penetrating analysis of this scene:

*Among all the disciples, Peter was the one who had protested his devotion to Jesus most vehemently, promising to follow him even to death (John 13.37). But he had three times denied his Lord, and it was he – apparently – who had led the flight from Jerusalem back to the old life of fishing (John 21.1). Now he is face to face with the friend he has denied and abandoned. Once again, as on that night of threefold apostasy, Jesus looks at him across a charcoal fire. Three times Jesus presses the simple yet painfully searching question 'Do you love me?' The question is not addressed to 'Peter', for the rock has proved an unstable quicksand. The disciple is addressed by his old name, the name he had before Jesus met and called him by the lakeside: 'Simon, son of John, do you love me more than these?'*

*Three times Peter answers with an affirmation of his love – but an affirmation which rests its confidence not on the strength of his own love but on the sureness of Jesus' knowledge. 'You know everything; you know that I love you.'*

Lesslie Newbigin, from *The Light Has Come* p. 278

This scene has an intensely personal quality about it. At the start of the conversation we read that Peter was excited – he could not wait for the boat to make its leisurely way to shore, so he jumped in the water and waded in. But surely he must also have felt ashamed, still broken in spirit from his experience of denial. However, by the end of the encounter I imagine a very changed Peter, now equipped, through his experience of brokenness and restoration, to become the leader he was called to be. And both the brokenness and restoration were necessary.

One of the authenticating features of the gospels is that they never conceal the failings of the disciples. No other ideology I have encountered can cope with the notion that its heroes were fallible, whether Lenin, the Ayatollah Khomeini, or Kim il Sung of North Korea. But in descriptions of the disciples, as with many of the Old Testament heroes of faith, there is a transparent honesty, not to let the reader gloat at human weakness, but rather to rejoice in the love and mercy of God in dealing with it. If God can forgive these people, then he can also forgive me, and deal with the failures and sins which distort and diminish my life.

If this were no more than a scene of reconciliation and forgiveness, it would still be amongst the most remarkable of the gospels. But I believe there is still more to it. When Peter and the other disciples come to the breakfast, they also contribute to it because Jesus asked them to: 'Jesus

said to them, "Bring some of the fish you have just caught" '
(John 21.10). In other words, Jesus asked them to bring something of themselves, their personalities and human skills, the
fruit of their hard work. Even the risen Lord asks for human
co-operation: the meal was not complete until Peter brought
his fish. Only after the co-operative breakfast is Peter told to 'go,
feed my lambs'. What Peter brings – what each of us brings –
to the service of Yeshua, is used by God to feed his flock.

*Do you love me?*

*You know that I do*

*Follow me then, wherever I go*

*Feed my lambs, feed my lambs*

# For Listening

## Day of Atonement/Lamb of God CD1

After the troubled instrumental music of Day of
Atonement, the choir voices the prayer 'grant us your
peace', only for the disquieting music to erupt again. The
events of Gethsemane and Calvary happened once for all:
the sins of the world were borne, forgiveness was made
possible, and a new Covenant forged. But the cry for
peace, and the need for atonement, will go on as long as
human beings find themselves estranged from God, from
their neighbour, and from themselves.

## Feed my Lambs CD1

*Masada*

# chapter **eight**

*Jesus left the temple and was walking away when his disciples came up to him to call his attention to the buildings. 'Do you see all these buildings?' he asked. 'I tell you the truth, not one stone here will be left on another; every one will be thrown down.'* (Matthew 24.1-2)

In A.D. 70 Jesus' prophetic words were fulfilled. For years there had been a gradual deterioration in the relations between the Jews and the Roman authorities, ruled by a succession of procurators whose chief ability seems to have been to offend Jewish religious and national sentiment. In A.D. 66 matters came to a head when the procurator Florus seized seventeen talents from the Temple treasury, an act of sacrilege that provoked a riot which was only put down with considerable bloodshed. Things went from bad to worse as full-blown rebellion developed. Even the strong reinforcements which arrived under the command of Cestus Gallus, Governor of Syria, failed to quell the insurrection but were forced to retreat in disarray, suffering heavy losses in the pass of Beth-Horon.

This early success undoubtedly filled the Jewish freedom-fighters with optimism. But it was short-lived. Vespasian, the Roman General entrusted with the task of putting down the rebellion, did so with methodical efficiency. Starting in Galilee, he picked off the centres of the revolt one by one. By the end of A.D. 69 only Jerusalem and three strongholds overlooking the Dead Sea were left, the most famous of which was the formidable hill-top fortress of Masada.

The walls of Jerusalem were breached in the spring of A.D. 70 and, despite furious resistance by the defenders, the Romans gradually captured more and more of the city until on July 24th the Antonia fortress was stormed. On August 29th the Temple was set on fire and destroyed. Four weeks later the whole city, with the exception of three towers of Herod's palace and part of the western wall of the Temple, was razed to the ground. The second great cycle of exile and return had begun, and was not to end until the creation of the State of Israel nearly 2,000 years later.

As we have seen, Judah Halevi's poem *To Israel in Exile* which we looked at in the context of the Babylonion Exile, was written at the mid-point of this long exile. I believe that, for anyone reading it today, this poem takes on powerful meanings which Halevi could not have anticipated. Despite his personal experience of persecution, he could not have envisaged the utter horror of the Holocaust. Despite his passion for Zion, he could not have foreseen the re-birth of the state of Israel.

I do not think we shall ever understand the significance of either of these events without first coming to terms with what it means to be in exile. What must it have meant to the survivors of the death camps, to the dispossessed remnant of the destroyed Jewish communities, and to their relatives overseas, to hear the call to 'come home, come back' after nearly 2,000 years of exile?

Those of us who live towards the end of a century which saw the systematic murder of six million Jews in the Shoah, which we call the Holocaust, are confronted by these issues in a new and terrible way. Even after spending much of the past ten years of my creative life considering the Holocaust, I still believe that it is virtually impossible for Gentiles to understand its impact on Jewish people, on their spirituality and culture, and on their understanding of their long exile and their recent return to the land.

Just after we recorded the music of *City of Peace*, the media began to report on the 50th anniversaries of the liberation of the Nazi extermination camps in 1944 and 1945. For fifty years many people, not only Jews, have asked the question, 'where was God in Auschwitz?', a question I too have sought to address with as much integrity as I can muster. Indeed, I think this is a question that should be addressed by all humanity, and certainly by all Christians. For until we understand how God can be present in utter darkness, how can we begin to understand the enormity of Jesus' journey on the cross into the depths of hell itself?

Two of the songs in *Song of an Exile* were based on poems written in Terezin, which as Theresienstadt was promoted in Nazi propaganda as the 'model Jewish ghetto'. The reality was different. In 1995, during a tour of the Czech Republic, I visited Terezin and came away with a visual image printed deep in my imagination. From the car, the first sight to hit the eyes is a very large cross, which stands in front of the memorial ground. Beyond that, and just outside the outer wall of the ghetto, there stands a large iron Star of David, which was placed there not long before my visit as part of the anniversary commemorations. As I walked along the path which leads into Terezin, the Cross and Star of David became aligned with each other. The result was the creation of a new image, which immediately conveyed to me the sense of Jesus suffering with his people the Jews, of Yeshua as having been with every man, woman and child that died in Terezin and Auschwitz and Belsen and Sobibor and all the rest.

*Memorial plaque at the Children's memorial site in Yad Vashem*

In a recent HTV programme about our performance of *Song of an Exile* in Yad Vashem in August 1994, Rabbi Hugo Gryn said something which transforms our question and gives it added meaning and power. His words have an authority which can only be claimed by someone who survived the extermination camps:

*Something monstrous happened at the heart of Western civilisation. There was an enormous act of betrayal of God, of religious tradition. And when that happens, almost anything and everything becomes thinkable and then do-able. And that is what happened there... I often hear the question, 'Where was God in Auschwitz?', and actually it's the wrong question. The real question has to be, 'Where was man in Auschwitz? What happened to humanity?'*

●●●●●

## The Journey Home

In many ways Ezekiel is the most disturbing – even frightening – of all Biblical prophets. In his words God's anger is laid bare, and the proclamation of his judgment highlights the consequences of the failure of the children of Israel to follow his law. Just as the Old Testament is honest in its refusal to conceal the failures and weaknesses of its heroes – David is the most obvious example – so there is a terrible honesty about the way in which God's passion for his people and his refusal to accept their half-hearted repentance are expressed. Yet there is a paradox. Alongside the declaration of judgment is the promise of forgiveness; juxtaposed with threats of punishment are words of tenderness and compassion.

Furthermore, deeply woven into the fabric of this prophecy is the utter humiliation, shame and lack of dignity of God's people as they travel through the nations, exiles from their promised land, separated from God. But there is also the sense that God shares in the shame of his people, and that he suffers as a consequence of their failure to obey his laws. God shares their exile, and speaks of his name being blasphemed and mocked by the peoples of the nations. They look at the exiled Jews and say, in effect, 'So you are the people of Yahweh; you are the people to whom this God gave the land. Now look at you. So much for your God!' The more I studied Ezekiel, the more I realized that God's faithfulness to his exiled people had to be outworked in their return to the land that God had given them. It had to be thus, not only as a sign that God has forgiven them, but also – and equally important – that his name may once again be glorified and esteemed by the nations.

*Again the word of the LORD came to me: 'Son of man, when the people of Israel were living in their own land, they defiled it by their conduct and the actions... So I poured out my wrath on them because they had shed blood in the land and because they had defiled it with their idols. I dispersed them among the nations and they were scattered through the countries; I judged them according to their conduct and their actions. And wherever they went among the nations they profaned my holy name, for it was said of them, "These are the LORD's people, and yet they had to leave his land". I had concern for my holy name, which the house of Israel profaned among the nations where they had gone.*

*Therefore say to the house of Israel, 'This is what the Sovereign LORD says: It is not for your sake, O house of Israel, that I am going to do these things, but for the sake of my holy name, which you have profaned among the nations where you have gone. I will show the holiness of my great name, which has been profaned among the nations, the name you have profaned among them. Then the nations will know that I am the LORD, declares the Sovereign LORD, when I show myself holy through you before their eyes.*

*For I will take you out of the nations; I will gather you from all the countries and bring you back into your own land. I will sprinkle clean water on you, and you will be clean; I will cleanse you from all your impurities and from all your idols. I will give you a new heart and put a new Spirit within you; I will remove from you your heart of stone and give you a heart of flesh. And I will put my Spirit in you and move you to follow my decrees and be faithful to keep my laws. You will live in the land I gave your forefathers; you will be my people, and I will be your God.* (Ezekiel 36.16-28)

If ever we ask why God chooses to act in the way that he does, these words must be at least part of the answer. God's desire to save his people is matched by his faithfulness. For Jews this may involve a physical return to 'the land', but for the rest of us it cannot involve less than a conscious, willing return to God from wherever or however we have been in exile – spiritual or physical – to the place of security, salvation and shalom. 'Come, let us return unto the Lord our God'.

I believe we must hold on to the truth that the call to return is addressed to all God's children, to all humanity. How else can we understand the core message of the New Testament that 'God in the Messiah was reconciling the world to himself' (2 Corinthians 5:19); that God chose to exile himself in order to search out all those who had exiled themselves from him, to heal our brokenness, and to bring us home.

# For Reflection

*Where I wander - you!  Where I ponder - you!*
*Only you, you again, always you!*


*When I'm gladdened - you!  When I'm saddened - you!*
*Only you, you again, always you!*


*Sky is you, earth is you*
*You above, you below*
*In every trend, at every end,*
*Only you, you again, always you!*


*You, You, You, You!*

Levi Yizchak (c. 1700)


In his foreword to my book *Children of Exile*, Rabbi Hugo Gryn introduced me to this poem: 'Du is a Yiddish word which means "You!" and its title is simply *A Dudele* - "a little You song". It was written about two hundred years ago by Levi Yizchak of Berdichev – and I have the feeling that he and Adrian Snell would have understood each other perfectly'.  He was right.  With its conscious awareness of the presence of God in all places and at all times, this simple yet beautiful poem is redolent of some of the prayers of the Celtic tradition which have been rediscovered in recent years and which are enriching Western spirituality once again.

In a sense, this poem is a reminder that, from first to last, we are confronted by the God who called himself I AM, and who is present in every place and at every stage of our lives:

*Where can I go from your Spirit?*
*Where can I flee from your presence?*
*If I go up to the heavens, you are there;*
*if I make my bed in the depths, you are there.*
*If I rise on the wings of the dawn,*
*if I settle on the far side of the sea,*
*even there your hand will guide me,*
*your right hand will hold me fast.*

(Psalm 139.7-10)

*You* could have been sung by heroes of faith like Abraham and Simon Peter. *You* is the story of their lives, and of many faithful Jews and Christians. Abraham's daily life was lived in the context of *You*. He had learned to live in contentment, with God in all things. In these words, Levi Yizchak is very close to the confident faith of St Patrick's Breastplate, the great 5th century Irish hymn. In the extract given below, I have substituted the Hebrew name for Jesus for the 'Christ' of the familiar translation.

*Yeshua be with me, Yeshua within me,*
*Yeshua behind me, Yeshua before me,*
*Yeshua beside me, Yeshua to win me,*
*Yeshua to comfort and restore me.*

*Yeshua beneath me, Yeshua above me,*
*Yeshua in quiet, Yeshua in danger,*
*Yeshua in hearts of all who love me,*
*Yeshua in mouth of friend and stranger.*

## For Listening

**You**  CD 1

*Flags at the Citadel*

# chapter **nine**

At last we are confronted with the issues which link modern Israel with Old Testament prophecy, the physical return to the land which is promised in Ezekiel chapter 36 and the spiritual return to God which Scripture sees as an integral part of any homecoming.  In addressing these questions I am conscious that I am wandering into at least two minefields.

First, it is clear Christian opinion has been polarised by the circumstances under which this return to the land has taken place, and all that has flowed from it.  Some see the return to Israel as part of God's plan.  This is certainly how my Messianic Jewish friends understand it, as well as many Christian groups in the West.   So the Synod of the Reformed Church in the Netherlands affirmed:

*In our time many Jews have again gone to the land of Palestine...precisely in its concrete visibility, this return points to the special significance of this people in the midst of the nations, and to the saving faithfulness of God...Therefore we rejoice in this reunion of people and land.  This reunion creates problems, poses enigmas, challenges many of our preconceptions.  Yet within this reunion and renewed Covenant lies the opportunity for reconciliation between Muslim, Christian and Jew, a potential blessing for all nations and, above all, the mysterious, awesome presence of Almighty God.*

On the other hand, others question whether Old Testament prophecies about a return to the land still reflect the purposes of God.  Are we to understand these words as God's will for the geopolitical reality of the Middle East today?  And if this is part of God's purposes, how can we reconcile this with the attitudes and actions of some of the returned exiles towards those who were already in the land in 1948?

I can only speak for myself. I believe we are seeing in our lifetime the partial fulfilment of these prophecies in the return of the Jewish people to Israel. I also believe that true peace will come to Yerushalayim when the people of Israel acknowledge Yeshua as Lord and Messiah, and his kingdom is established forever, which the Bible promises will come one day:

*And when he appeared as a human being, he humbled himself still more by becoming obedient even to death - death on a stake as a criminal! Therefore God raised him to the highest place and gave him the name above every name; that in honour of the name given Yeshua, every knee will bow – in heaven, on earth and under the earth – and every tongue will acknowledge that Yeshua the Messiah is Adonai – to the glory of God the Father.* (Philippians 2. 5-11, *Jewish New Testament*)

If God had to exile his people because of their rebellion, and then brought them back because of his holy name, then we cannot avoid asking hard questions of him. In particular, if we think of the long exile which began in AD70 and ended in 1948, not only was the name of the God of Abraham, Isaac and Jacob profaned in the nations, but the Jewish people themselves were mocked, despised, persecuted and killed, not least as a result of a distorted theology which gave spurious justification for regarding the Jews as a 'has-been' people. We've already encountered the question 'Where was God in Auschwitz?' Are we now to ask, 'Where was God throughout the diaspora?'

This is our next minefield. Throughout this period, much of the Christian Church developed a whole theology which saw the Jews as 'Christ-killers', cursed by God and ripe for summary punishment. Fostered by some whom we regard as spiritual giants – men like St John Chrysostom and Martin Luther – this attitude was to deepen immeasurably the divide between the Christian Church and the faith from which it developed. And behind it lies a yet more perplexing question: 'What did God think he was doing, letting the followers of Yeshua persecute the children of Abraham?'

•••••

While writing this chapter, news came through of yet another terrorist bombing in Jerusalem, killing twenty-five people on a bus (including the Hamas member who planted it), injuring many more, and jeopardising the fragile peace process between the Israeli government and the Palestine Liberation Organisation. Recently Prime Minister Rabin has been assassinated, by a Jew, an event unforeseen by the formidable Israeli security services and un-dreamed of by the Israeli people. In this utterly volatile atmosphere the issues raised are so complex, so governed by media-influenced impressions, and so dangerously open to snap judgment and simplistic analysis, that to be able to give a balanced view one needs to be expert – politically, socially, historically – in a way that I could never claim to be.

However, the political and social issues are so interwoven with the religious questions that they cannot be avoided. Indeed, no Christian can, with integrity, consider these matters and ignore the 1947 United Nations Partition Plan, the Six Day

War, the recapture of Jerusalem, settlement policies in the occupied territories, the treatment of the Palestinians in the state of Israel, Palestinian self-determination in Gaza and the West Bank, or any of the other elements in the recent history of the Land.

I am well aware that the way events in Israel are generally reported has led to a general perception - not least by Christians in the West - of Israel as a harsh, even brutal, oppressor of a dispossessed minority. Christians, of course, must be passionately concerned with justice for all the people of the land and compassion for those of its people who are disadvantaged or oppressed. But justice and compassion need to be informed, and I believe we in the West have tended to receive an over-simplified picture of this complex situation. If we want to correct this over-simplification we shall need to keep in a mind a number of facts and issues which are often forgotten, but which in part lie at the root of the present conflicts.

For example, we should remember that in accepting the United Nations Partition Plan, the founding fathers of Israel agreed to the concept of an independent sovereign Palestinian state. It was the Arab leadership which refused to accept this Partition Plan, choosing instead to seek the destruction of the emergent state of Israel, by launching a *Jihad*, or holy war, against her. I am, however, fully aware that the Arabs themselves saw this as a defensive campaign, with the intention of liberating the Palestinians from this new political state whose creation they saw as in itself an act of war.

Therefore, within days of the 15th May 1948 Declaration of Independence of the state of Israel, the Grand Mufti of Jerusalem, a supporter of the Nazis during World War II, along with the Arab High Command, ordered a temporary evacuation of Palestine to give the five invading Arab armies greater freedom when they attacked Israel. When the Arab forces were defeated, against all expectations, those Palestinian evacuees were left stranded. Unwanted by the 'host' nations, this brought about the crises of the West Bank and Gaza refugee camps; UN resolutions, claims and counter claims and of course much human suffering have followed ever since.

Further, at the conclusion of the Six Day War – started by Syria in 1967 with the aim of the destruction of Israel, and during which the Golan heights were captured – Israel offered the Gaza strip and other territorial compromises in return for guaranteed peace. The response of the Arab states was 'No peace with Israel, no negotiations with Israel, no recognition of Israel' (Khartoum Arab Summit, August 1967).

And perhaps the most seemingly insoluble dilemma, drawing as it does on the most fundamental and deeply held beliefs, where compromise is out of the question – indeed would be an act of religious betrayal – the reality that for Jews to have a state on any part of the Islamic Middle East is an anathema to Islam.

*Jews, like Christians, have to be tolerated traditionally within the Islamic Empire, but only on condition of remaining subjugated as second class* (dhimmi) *citizens. Now, for the first time, the unthinkable has happened; a* dhimmi *people has become independent and a formerly Islamic land has reverted to its pre-Islamic, Jewish faith. Such a development is, for Islam, unforgivable.*

Dr. Margaret Brearly, from *A Christian response to the Middle East*

We should not forget that the freedom enjoyed by the world's press in Israel today means that the disturbances, of the Intifada for example, are broadcast in vivid detail with the excesses of some Israeli soldiers captured on film for all the world to see. But we remain largely in the dark over the many civil rights abuses, the oppression and violence elsewhere in the Middle East. We should remember when those countries give vocal support to the cause of the Palestinians, that their laws would not permit either Palestinian Christians or Jews to practise their faith with anything like the freedom enjoyed by non-Jews in Israel.

Complex issues indeed, and no simple solutions. Jerusalem, which for centuries has had to live with the tensions inherent in being a city sacred to Jews, Christians and Muslims, is today the focal point of political disagreement between the Israeli and Palestinian authorities, each of which claims it as their capital. Mix the spiritual and political claims, coupled with the extremists intentions on all sides, and it is hard to avoid the conclusion that Israel will face difficult times ahead. Some of my close friends there are anxious about the prospect of further conflict before the end of the millennium. They may be right, though the thought of further destruction within this much-loved country and carnage amongst its peoples is too terrible to contemplate. These prophetic words from Zechariah ring only too true:

*Behold I am going to make Jerusalem a cup that causes reeling to all the peoples around...* (Zechariah 12, 2 *New American Standard Bible*)

We must remember too, that whenever we discuss Israel we are dealing with a nation whose government, just like any government, including our own, is fallible, with the capacity to make good and bad decisions. They have learned, however, not to have absolute faith in any other country or its government, because history has showed them that they dare

*The Wailing Wall and the Dome of the Rock...*

*Crossing the Lebanon border*

not. The centuries of isolation and persecution in scattered communities throughout the world, particularly in Europe, have now been succeeded by a half-century in which the people of Israel are still experiencing isolation. Israel is confronted by twenty-two Islamic states, only two of which, Egypt and Jordan, are officially at peace with her. Perhaps it should come as no surprise that there exists within Israel a degree of protectionism, a lack of trust, and an almost tangible fear about the real motives of some Palestinian leaders. At the time of writing, the 1964 PLO charter, which calls for the destruction of Israel, has still not been renounced, although Yasser Arafat has pledged himself to renounce it as part of the current peace accords with Israel.

I cannot imagine what it must be like to live in such a volatile environment. If we in the West had had to face a similar situation, after nearly 2,000 years of exile culminating in a communal experience as catastrophic as the Holocaust, would we be any less distrustful of others, and determined to remain defensively strong?

In these chapters we have considered the horrors of the Shoah and the complex political realities of the state of Israel. Rabbi Lionel Blue, writing in *To Heaven with Scribes and Pharisees*, shows how they are inter-related:

*What is the meaning of the destruction of European Jewry, and the rise of Israel? For Jews these are not just human affairs, to be given sociological explanations, which always look so neat after the event. These events are like the Exodus, and the destruction of the Temple. A force has hurled Judaism into a new trajectory. It is not easy to say more. Among ordinary Jewish people, interpretations are already taking place, without the help of intellectuals or rabbis. They are simple, potent, and possibly dangerous. For some the destruction of European Jewry was the punishment for assimilation, for being lured into the gentile world, for selling the Jewish inheritance, and birthright. For others, God took away six million dead, and Israel is the holy compensation. Jews are very sensitive about Israel. On its existence hinges the justice of God made visible in events.*

My own view, which I believe to be supported by observers of contemporary Israeli society, is that as the Jewish people return to a land where, for the first time since AD70, they feel themselves to be truly at home, so the security provided by that homecoming has encouraged many Israelis of every age and background to consider new ideas in a way which till now would have been impossible. Of course, this openness can have both positive and negative results. Israel has its own proliferation of cults and New Age movements, no doubt (as in the West) in reaction to the secularism and materialism which are so evident in their society.

But there are also Messianic Jews. It is a commonly-voiced belief within Messianic circles that behind the creation of the State of Israel and subsequent events is a deeper purpose: the revelation to this people of who Yeshua is. In Israel there are around forty Messianic congregations, including at least seven Hebrew-speaking congregations in Jerusalem itself. I have heard it suggested that there are a growing number of secret believers amongst the rabbis – the successors of Nicodemus – who are discovering who Messiah is and are allowing that discovery gradually to come forth in their ideas and teaching, without making public statements about it which would exclude them from their congregations.

The cycle of judgment and mercy, exile and return, remains a great mystery. Is it beyond the bounds of possibility that we shall see the fulfilment of all this in our lifetime? Is the hour for the revelation of Yeshua as Messiah to the Jewish people and to the world at hand?

# chapter **ten**

The Jerusalem of today's news bulletins, and the circumstances in which its citizens worship, work, play and live out their daily lives, are not the final chapter of this city's story. Today's reality fails to do justice to the vision of the New Jerusalem and God's promises regarding its place in the redemption of the world. For that reason, the final section of *City of Peace* points to the realisation of those promises, and the joyful return of his children, restored and redeemed, into the presence of the Father.

But how to convey the richness and the depth of meaning, the nobility, grace and wonder of the vision of Jerusalem, as conceived in the mind and will of God? Only a prophet, a poet or – perhaps – a musician can hope to convey something of that vision. Even the last chapters of St John the Divine's apocalyptic vision of the Holy City rely on symbol and colourful imagery to describe the New Jerusalem.

The title-song of *City of Peace* returns in a simple way to some of those promises, spread throughout the Jewish Bible but seen in perhaps their clearest form in Isaiah.

*And this is my song to Jerusalem*

*No city on earth so fair*

*Your wounds are as deep and as wide as the sea*

*But no jewel was ever so rare*

*Your gold gleams bright through refiner's fire*

Your heart beats ever with mine
O City of Peace shall at last be true
Your vineyards shall flow with wine

And those who rage against you
Shall be as nothing at all
For I shall be always before you
And you shall answer my call
O comfort, comfort my people
Comfort with tender words
The time for mourning is over
No more weeping shall be heard

Now hear a voice of one calling
Prepare a way for the King
Make straight a path in the desert
For he has great tidings to bring

For the people who walked in darkness
Have seen a new day dawn
For unto us a Son is given
And to us a child is born
And his kingdom shall last forever
The City of Peace shall dance
To the rhythm and song of the flute and the drum
As the celebration starts

## City of Peace - Yerushalayim

*Our eyes can see mercy flow like a river*
*Love the Lord your God with all your strength and might*
*With all your heart and soul my people come*
*Teach my laws for life to your children*
*And walk with the words of life all around you*
*Every hope, every word, every promise,*
*every dream has come true*

based on passages from Isaiah

What a glorious vision! The city and the people at peace in the promised day of the Lord, the day of the Son who has been given, of the child who has been born in fulfilment of prophecy. As they and we acknowledge his kingdom, the celebration starts and the dance of salvation can begin. Each of us who enters into the life of God has a vital part to play in that dance, though I recognise from my own life that our steps will always falter this side of eternity. But it is 'the dance', and we shall step out unembarrassed by past failures and inadequacies, unencumbered by achievements, status or skills, but with the unselfconscious exuberance and simplicity of a child.

This is emphasised in *Children of the Dream*, which recalls the deliverance of God's people from the captivity of exile. It is based on Psalm 126, one of the songs which pilgrims sang on their way up to Jerusalem.

*When the Lord returned again*
*the captive ones to Zion*
*we were children of the dream.*
*Our mouths were filled with laughter*
*and our tongues with songs of joy –*
*we are children of the dream.*

*Then did all the nations say*
*'The LORD has done great things –*
*they are children of the dream'*

*Lord restore our fortunes*
*as the desert and the stream*
*we are children of the dream.*

*Those who sow in tears*
*O they shall reap at harvest time –*
*they are children of the dream,*
*they are children of the dream.*

based on Psalm 126

The return of the people to Zion has become a sign to all
the nations of the greatness of the God who has restored his
people to their home and assured them of his presence. No
longer is the Lord's name profaned or mocked. The power of
these words is all the greater if we are able to understand exile
as more than physical separation from land or city, but as a

spiritual condition. Then these words can be sung by people of all nationalities with all the excitement and exuberance of the original Psalm, as we sing of our joyful return from spiritual exile to God.

The poem is called *Children of the Dream*, because I wanted to add an important feature to the original Psalm, not from a desire to re-write Scripture but to introduce an important gospel insight to this song of return:

*At that time the disciples asked came to Jesus and asked 'Who is the greatest in the kingdom of heaven?' He called a little child and had him stand among them. And he said: 'I tell you the truth, unless you change and become like little children, you will never enter the kingdom of God. Therefore, whoever humbles himself like this child is the greatest in the kingdom of heaven.'* (Matthew 18. 1-5)

We find the same point in the following chapter, where St Matthew relates one of the most touching scenes in Jesus' ministry:

*People were also bringing babies to Jesus for him to place his hands on them and pray for them to have him touch them. But the disciples rebuked those who brought them. Jesus said, 'Let the little children come to me, and do not hinder them, for the kingdom of God belongs to such as these.'* (Matthew 19. 13-14)

In Luke's version, Jesus makes the same point even more forcefully:

*'I tell you the truth anyone who will not receive the kingdom of God like a little child will never enter it.'* (Luke 18.17)

When Jesus told his disciples to become like children, he was not referring to the more negative aspects of childhood which any parent – or, indeed, most other children – would recognise. Rather, he was encouraging the disciples, and through them all who follow him, to rediscover in themselves those qualities which are characteristic of childhood, but which are so often fatally stifled as we get older: trust, wide-eyed wonder, innocent joy, a sense of dependence, open receptivity, and enthusiasm, in the best, deepest sense of the word. It is widely recognised that these qualities develop as the child experiences unqualified love and devoted care. It is as we receive these same gifts from God that we are able to rediscover the essentially quality of childhood which fits us for his presence.

To think of children is to look to the future, to the fulfilment of promise and the transformation of potential into achievement. So the realisation that we are 'children of the dream' is testimony to the fact that the promises of God will be fulfilled. We are also used to the idea of the child as an heir, which St Paul explores in his letter to the Romans:

*'For you did not receive a spirit that makes you a slave again to fear, but you received the Spirit of sonship. And by him we cry, "Abba, Father". The Spirit himself testifies with our spirit that we are God's children. Now if we are children, then we are heirs - heirs of God and co-heirs with Christ...'* .                                    (Romans 8.15- 17a)

The 'children of the dream' share in the inheritance which the Father has promised for all who love him.

In *Like a Child*, which is based on Psalm 131, we are reminded that alongside the cosmic view of salvation history and its fulfilment we must always place the intimacy with which God loves us and assures us of his presence.

*Three weeks old*

*O Lord, my heart is not lifted up*

*My eyes are not raised too high*

*I do not occupy myself with things*

*Too great and too marvellous for me*

*But I have calmed and quieted my soul*

*Like a child that is quieted at its mother's breast*

*Like a child that is quieted is my soul*

*O Israel hope in the Lord from this time forth*

*And for evermore...*

Psalm 131

For me, the most important part of the text comes in lines 5 and 6, with the image of the child nestling in the calm security of its mother's breast. The text of the Psalm makes it clear that the child is already weaned, no longer dependent on the mother for physical nourishment. Therefore, the image is of the kind of embrace, familiar to any loving mother, which comes perhaps at the end of the day or at a time of distress or insecurity, when the young child simply wants to be held in the place of safety, peace and unconditional love.

The words in those two lines have more personal significance for me than all the weighty issues, discussions and debates. More important is the experience of the love of God our Father who 'tends his flock like a shepherd; he gathers the lambs in his arms and carries them close to his heart; he gently leads those that have young' (Isaiah 40.11).

'We may our ends by our beginnings show' - so wrote Sir John Denham in the 17th century. Something of that is expressed in the final stanza of *City of Peace,* which links in the glorious vision of the New Jerusalem with the Shema Yisrael –

143

the 'words for life' which God gave to Israel, the 'laws for life' which are to be impressed on our children, to be taken from the mind into the heart. This well-spring of the Jewish faith is present in the foundations of the New Jerusalem, the place of the perfect shalom made possible by the death and resurrection of Yeshua, the Way, the Truth and the Life, the Prince of Peace.

> *Shema Yisrael*
> *The Lord is One.*
> *His dominion is without limit,*
> *boundless in space, endless in time.*
> *Adonai ehad.*
>
> *God's unity encompasses life and death,*
> *heaven and earth, light and darkness.*
> *The Lord is One,*
> *the sum of all that has been,*
> *the promise of all that is to be.*
> *Adonai ehad.*
>
> *God's Oneness unites us with nature,*
> *the smallest grain of sand with the farthest star.*
> *The Lord is one.*
> *God's unity is sensed in the struggle*
> *for human harmony, for harmony with nature.*
> *Adonai ehad.*
>
> *We make God's purposes our own*
> *when we dedicate body and soul to His service,*
> *when we attain that love of other creatures*
> *which is at one with the love of God.*

Rabbi Gershon Hadas (1897-1980), from *Siddur Sim Shalom* p.815

# For Reflection

## Shalom

*Come into my life and make this house your home – Shalom*
*Breathe my fragrance, drink my wine, O sleep in joy – Shalom*
*Friend embrace this maiden, feel her brightness like the sun*
*Come closer, touch her lips and let this sweetness be Shalom*

*By your life, my love, revive me*
*Kiss my lips, restore, inspire me*
*O I have no love besides you*
*Always, only you – Shalom*

*Far away is my beloved, cling to me – Shalom*
*She will not be back tomorrow, but rest assured – Shalom*
*And when I lay my eyes upon you, safe again – Shalom*

based on an anonymous Yemenite poem

This anonymous Yemenite poem is about the joyful intimacy of two lovers, and was originally read or sung at a wedding, addressed by the bride to her beloved. Here it is used in an attempt to circumvent some of the comfortable, over-familiar expressions we tend to associate with shalom, and instead to let it speak to our imaginations with new power and directness.

The shalom which we know to be ours through faith is here revealed in its fulness as part of the final consummation of the City of Peace. As the momentum picks up towards that final revelation, so we discover more of the power behind shalom: wholeness of life, utter security, true well-being, oneness with God and neighbour, everything that is good and a blessing. All this is God's intention for us as individuals, as families, as communities and nations. It was always his intention for Israel that his people would live in shalom and that out of shalom would come generous hospitality, a welcome for foreigners and the stranger within the gates, a shalom which would bless them and send them on still blessed.

I believe that God intends once again to make Israel a place of true shalom, though that will come to pass only in God's good time. Just as perfect love casts out fear, so when true shalom comes there will be no need for protectionism or for any mistreatment of foreigners and strangers. The nation will be at one with itself, whole, able to extend the hand of friendship to all and bring to completion the promises which are enshrined in the name of its capital: Yerushalayim - the City of Peace.

# For Listening

**Children of the Dream** CD2

**Like a Child** CD2

**Shalom** CD2

**City of Peace** CD2

# coda

*We cannot let go of each other*
*not he of me nor I of him*

The promises will be fulfilled, and those who know the living God have already received a foretaste of that fulfilment. It would have been possible to stop there, and to end *City of Peace* on this rapturous 'high'. Possible, but dishonest. For while we must hold ever before us the vision of what will be, we must come back down to earth, to the reality of our own lives, of the world in which we live, and of Jerusalem today.

When I was doing some research for *City of Peace*, I came across a poem by Aaron Zeitlin which, to my mind, explores the mystery of the relationship between God and humanity in a special way. In particular, it considers the complex relationship between the Jewish people and God, how they understand his judgment and mercy, how they are able to relate to God even after Auschwitz and Belsen and Majdanek and Sobibor and Terezin. Because the poem was too long to use in its entirety, I abbreviated it into a form which could act as a postlude to *City of Peace*.

*If I become a storm*
*or if I blaze in rebellion against Him*
*is He not still the one who, bleeding in my wounds,*
*my cries still praise, my cries still praise?*

*Can I then choose, even now*
*not to believe in Him*
*for only to Him, only to Him*
*can I cry out the cry of every vein and limb*

*Because He lives and wills*
*because He does not sleep in rigid law*
*I cannot understand his deeds*
*at His feet my ashes lie*

*We cannot let go of each other*
*not He of me, nor I of Him*
*You say 'Israel' when you say 'Elohim'*

*I believe He suffers with me*
*if I cry out against Him*
*with me he cries*

*He who commands the destroyer*
*to set my house on fire*
*wishes to reward and crown me*
*with His most dazzling crown.*

based on a poem by Aaron Zeitlin (1898 1973), from *A Treasury of Yiddish Poetry*

These words spoke to me very powerfully, and gave expression to many thoughts and emotions which have been part of my own pilgrimage in the three or so years during which *City of Peace* has dominated my creative life. Some of these have surfaced in this book, which is in many ways an intimate record of that personal journey.

For me, the fourth stanza of the song is crucial not only to this poem, nor even to *City of Peace,* but to the whole history of Yerushalayim. It refers to the incident when Jacob wrestled with God at Peniel.

*That night Jacob got up and took his two wives, his two maidservants and his eleven sons and crossed the ford of the Jabbok. After he had sent them across the stream, he sent over all his possessions. So Jacob was left alone, and a man wrestled with him till daybreak. When the man saw that he could not overpower him, he touched the socket of Jacob's hip so that his hip was wrenched as he wrestled with the man. Then the man said, 'Let me go, for it is daybreak.' But Jacob replied, 'I will not let you go unless you bless me.' The man asked him, 'What is your name?' 'Jacob', he answered. Then the man said, 'Your name will longer be Jacob, but Israel, because you have struggled with God and with men and have overcome.' Jacob said, 'Please tell me your name.' But he replied, 'Why do you ask me my name?' Then he blessed him there. So Jacob called the place Peniel, saying, 'It is because I saw God face to face, and yet my life was spared.'* (Genesis 32.22-30)

The name Israel means 'he struggles with God', and the struggle to believe, to hang on to God, sometimes the struggle to survive at all, has characterised the history of the Jewish people ever since their forefather was given his new name. This is, then, a profoundly Jewish poem in the way that it lets

*Gate to the garden of Gethsemane*

different aspects of the struggle of faith rise to the surface. The struggle between wanting to cry out at God in complaint or confusion, and realising that the One at whom I rail is the same God whom it is my every instinct to praise. The struggle to worship and serve a living God whose deeds are beyond human understanding, at whose feet 'my ashes lie' - surely Zeitlin must have had in mind the images of the Holocaust. The struggle to live through suffering, and yet to believe that God suffers with me.

This is not to ignore the ministry of Yeshua, or to diminish the saving power of the cross and the glory of the resurrection. Neither is it to wish away a proper, God-given assurance of salvation, nor to suggest for a moment that God is brought down by human pain. However, we begin to grasp the scale of human misery, the power of human anger that the world is still not as it will be, the depth of human frustration that the shalom for which we long with every fibre of our being is not yet a living reality. Only then can we begin to comprehend the scale of the love which chose to reach out towards humanity, to redeem the lost, the careless and the self-sufficient, and to make shalom. Only then can we glimpse the scale of the love and goodness of God, made known to us through Yeshua Ha-Moshiach, and brought to life in us by the Spirit who lives within us, interpreting to God those hopes, fears, struggles and longings which are too deep even to put into words.

One of the reasons I respond to this poem is because there are times when I find faith difficult: times when, although I know somehow that God is in my life, and that he is still with me, I end up asking myself if it might not be easier not to believe. The message of *I Believe* is that at the heart of the mystery of faith is a struggle, familiar to the Patriarchs, the

Prophets and to myriads more. The encouragement of this poem is that the fact that we struggle in faith should not worry us, for to be part of Israel, whether (to use Paul's imagery from Romans 11) as of the original olive branches or one of the ingrafted wild olive shoots, is to bear a name which means 'the one who struggles with God'. The challenge of this poem, which I believe is also the challenge of Yeshua's parable of the talents, is to stop hanging on to our past experience or our present faith, but to go on holding onto God, and God alone; for 'we cannot let go of each other, not He of me, nor I of Him'.

And the struggle goes on: for all who love Jerusalem, for all who live in the Land of the Holy One, and for all who will one day belong and live in shalom in the New Jerusalem.

# For Reflection

## The Peace of Jerusalem

Jerusalem is a witness, an echo of eternity. She is the city where waiting for God was born. Jerusalem is waiting for the prologue of redemption. She is the city where the hope for peace was born. Jerusalem inspires prayer: an end to rage and violence. She is holiness in history, memory and assurance. The stones of Jerusalem heard the promise of Isaiah: 'In time to come all people shall stream to Jerusalem, eager to learn of God's ways and to walk in his paths. For instruction comes from Zion, the word of the Lord from Jerusalem.'

Jerusalem's past is a prelude. She is never at the end of the road. Jerusalem is the promise of peace and God's presence. The work of the Lord from Jerusalem declares: 'They shall beat their swords into ploughshares, their spears into pruning hooks. Nation shall not lift sword against nation, nor shall they experience war anymore.' Jerusalem is the joy of the earth: may her peace and prosperity lead us to song. May we witness the peace of Jerusalem; may those who love her prosper. May we all be embraced by her promise: peace and God's presence. Amen.

Adapted from Dr Abraham Joshua Heschel, based on passages from Isaiah and the Psalms, *Siddur Sim Shalom* p. 817

# For Listening

## I Believe CD2

Adrian Snell's latest two album concept work *City of Peace* explores the Jewish roots of the Christian faith drawing on poems written by Jewish authors from six thousand years ago to the present day. The recordings unfold many themes including – the majesty and mystery of Jerusalem, the longing for Messiah, His coming and the promise of 'The City at peace forever'.

Available now from your local retailer

*Moriah* – City of Peace part 1 (ALD/ALC033)
*My Every Breath* – City of Peace part 2 (ALD/ALC03)

*Other works of Adrian include:*

| | |
|---|---|
| Children of Exile | Paperback & Hardcover |
| SOLO | CD & Music cassette |
| Beautiful... Or What?! | CD & Music cassette |
| Kiss the Tears | CD & Music cassette |
| Father | CD & Music cassette |
| We Want To Live | CD & Music cassette |
| Song of an Exile | CD & Music cassette |
| Alpha & Omega | CD & Music cassette |
| Feed the Hungry Heart | CD & Music cassette |
| The Passion | CD & Music cassette |
| Live at Flevo | VHS video |
| The Best of Adrian Snell | Songbook |
| The Passion | Songbook |

A Sheetmusic catalogue is also available.

All titles are available from your local christian retailer. In case of difficulty they may be ordered from The Music Works, Bath.

*Snell Mail* keeps you up to date with Adrian's work and concerts. If you would like your name added to the mailinglist, please write to the following address:

> The Music Works
> 11 Junction Road
> Oldfield Park
> Bath
> BA2 3NQ

# Monarch Publications
*Books of Substance*

All Monarch books can be purchased from your local Christian or general bookshop. In case of difficulty they may be ordered from the publisher:

Monarch Publications
Broadway House
The Broadway
Crowborough
East Sussex
TN6 1HQ

Please enclose a cheque payable to Monarch Publications for the cover price plus: 60p for the first book ordered plus 40p per copy for each additional book, to a maximum charge of £3.00 to cover postage and packing (UK and Republic of Ireland only).

Overseas customers please order from:

Christian Marketing PTY Ltd
PO Box 519
Belmont
Victoria 3216
Australia

Omega Distributors Ltd
69 Great South Road
Remuera
Auckland
New Zealand

Struik Christian Books
80 McKenzie Street Gardens
Cape Town 8001
South Africa

# Messianic Jews:
# The Search For Identity

## John Fieldsend

One of the most significant phenomena of the church today must be the growth of the Messianic Jewish movement – Jewish people who have come to realise that Jesus of Nazareth really is the Messiah of Israel and the Son of God.

Of course there have always been such Jewish people in our churches, but today we are seeing the commitment of many of them to develop their own congregations and lifestyle, based on their Jewishness as well as their New Testament faith. Is this dangerous, or exciting and appropriate?

In this important and very readable book John Fieldsend, himself a British Messianic Jewish leader, helps us to explore the beliefs and practices of Messianic Jews today. He covers the nature of contemporary Judaism, the objections for both Jews and Christians, the chief characteristics of Messianic Judaism, and the part it can play in shaping the future development of the Body of Christ.

Co-published with Olive Press.

ISBN 1 85424 228 8

£6.99

Monarch
Publications

# Yeshua Ben David

## Walter Riggans

### Why do the Jewish people reject Jesus as their Messiah?

Today many Jewish scholars and rabbis insist that Jesus could not have been the Messiah of Israel. This is not just a problem for those who wish to present the Christian faith to their Jewish friends. If Jesus is not the Messiah, neither is he the Christ! This denial of Jesus' credentials as Messiah strikes right at the foundations of the Christian faith.

In part one Walter Riggans considers the historical and theological backdrop to the debate. In the second part he focuses on specific texts and doctrines which present particular thorny issues. The underlying purpose is to reach out in love and understanding to our Jewish friends and neighbours. 'This book is not about easy Christian answers to difficult Jewish questions. It is about Jewish people, and how to help them really to meet Jesus, the Son of David.'

The Rev. Dr. Walter Riggans lived in Israel for nine years. He is Director General of the Church's Ministry Among Jewish People, and author of *The Covenant with the Jews* and *Jesus Ben Joseph.*

Co-published with Olive Press.

ISBN 1 85424 287 3

£10.99

Monarch
Publications

# Has God Finished With Israel?

## Rob Richards

For many years, Rob Richards has researched the place of Israel in purposes of God. This book describes how, with mounting excitement, he traced the links between the Old and New Testaments – 'we tend to start the Bible half-way through' – and considered what it meant and means to be the Chosen People.

In the process he unfolds what the Bible has to say about the covenants, the promised Messiah, the concept that Christians are heirs together with Israel, the Hebrew thinking behind so much of scripture, and much more. Rob concludes with a detailed look at what the future may hold in terms of the current political situation and the fulfilment of prophecy.

The Rev. Rob Richards was former UK Director of the Church's Ministry among Jewish People.

Co-published with Olive Press

ISBN 1 85424 243 1

£4.99

Monarch
Publications